The First Cities

LIFE WORLD LIBRARY
LIFE NATURE LIBRARY
TIME READING PROGRAM
THE LIFE HISTORY OF THE UNITED STATES
LIFE SCIENCE LIBRARY
GREAT AGES OF MAN
TIME-LIFE LIBRARY OF ART
TIME-LIFE LIBRARY OF AMERICA
FOODS OF THE WORLD
THIS FABULOUS CENTURY
LIFE LIBRARY OF PHOTOGRAPHY
THE TIME-LIFE ENCYCLOPEDIA OF GARDENING
THE AMERICAN WILDERNESS
THE EMERGENCE OF MAN
THE OLD WEST
FAMILY LIBRARY:
   THE TIME-LIFE BOOK OF FAMILY FINANCE
   THE TIME-LIFE FAMILY LEGAL GUIDE

TIME
LIFE
BOOKS ®

The Emergence of Man

The First Cities

by Dora Jane Hamblin
and the Editors
of Time-Life Books

Time-Life Books
New York

THE EMERGENCE OF MAN
SERIES EDITOR: Dale M. Brown
Editorial Staff for The First Cities:
Text Editor: Anne Horan
Picture Editor: Adrian C. Allen
Designer: Leonard Wolfe
Staff Writers: Paul Hathaway, Gerald Simons,
Timberlake Wertenbaker, Johanna Zacharias
Chief Researcher: Peggy Bushong
Researchers: Helen Greenway, Gail Hansberry,
Brenda Huff, Kumait Jawdat, Suad McCoy, Joann McQuiston,
Kathy Ann Ritchell, Carolyn Stallworth
Design Assistant: Jean Held

Editorial Production
Production Editor: Douglas B. Graham
Assistant: Gennaro C. Esposito
Quality Director: Robert L. Young
Assistant: James J. Cox
Copy Staff: Rosalind Stubenberg (chief), Charles Blackwell,
Nancy Houghtaling, Florence Keith
Picture Department: Dolores A. Littles, Marianne Dowell

Valuable aid was given by these departments and individuals
of Time Inc.: Editorial Production, Norman Airey,
Nicholas Costino Jr.; Library, Benjamin Lightman; Picture
Collection, Doris O'Neil; Photographic Laboratory, George Karas;
TIME-LIFE News Service, Murray J. Gart; Correspondents
Margot Hapgood, Anne Angus and Gail Ridgwell (London),
Ann Natanson (Rome), Maria Vincenza Aloisi and
Josephine du Brusle (Paris), Elisabeth Kraemer and Renee Houle
(Bonn), James Shepherd (New Delhi), Spencer Davidson (Beirut),
Ghulam Ahmed Nanji (Karachi), Mehmet Ali Kislali (Ankara).

The Author: DORA JANE HAMBLIN, for many years a staff member of LIFE, is a freelance writer who lives in Rome. She is the author of Pots and Robbers, a book about archeology in Italy, and is co-author of First Men on the Moon, based on her LIFE articles on the astronauts. For The First Cities, she traveled extensively in the Middle East to visit the sites of prehistoric communities.

The Consultant: C. C. LAMBERG-KARLOVSKY is Professor of Anthropology at Harvard University and Curator of Near Eastern Archaeology at the university's Peabody Museum. For the past seven summers he has been director of excavations of Tepe Yahya, a small city that began its existence 6,500 years ago in the hill country of southeastern Iran, some 60 miles north of the Arabian Sea.

The Cover: In one of the world's first cities, the 2500 B.C. metropolis of Moenjo-Daro in what today is Pakistan, residents go about their daily business. In the foreground, a woman carries home an earthenware jar of water drawn from a public well. Behind her, a vendor of clay figurines tries to interest a prospective buyer in his wares. Though the citizens of Moenjo-Daro left no complete record of how they dressed, archeologists surmise their clothing resembled present-day Pakistani garb. The figures were painted by Burt Silverman on a photograph of the surviving ruins of Moenjo-Daro.

Contents

Introduction

Man's curiosity about his origins inevitably leads him to ask how cities began. When, where and what were the first ones like, and why did they arise? What processes in the past were involved in man's transition from a hunter and gatherer to village dweller and eventually to citizen? In an attempt to find answers to these questions, 19th Century archeologists turned their attention to the cities of the Egyptian, Persian, Babylonian and Classical civilizations. But only since the Second World War have scholars begun to consider more seriously the prehistoric cities—the true first cities—on which these later civilizations were built. The new investigators have traced city life to at least 8000 B.C. and have, as well, greatly expanded its geographical range throughout Western Asia. This book reviews the dramatic advances they have made in recent years.

There is within the earliest cities a strange mixture of modern and archaic characteristics. At Jericho, as early as 10,000 years ago, the arts, crafts and architecture reflected achievements instantly recognizable as urban. In the later city-states of the Sumerian civilization, the patterns of daily life, class distinctions, military prowess, fashion, public pomp, slums, professional artisans, legal humbug and literary arts presage the urban world of the 20th Century, some 5,000 years in the future. But if many aspects of life there are familiar, others would seem unusual to the modern city dweller. Production depended almost entirely on human rather than animal or mechanical power, and the mass of the population was illiterate—in fact, in the earliest of these cities writing was unknown. People were resigned to dying young and to the possibility of such catastrophes as flash fires, sudden floods and epidemics.

In 1967, I conducted an archeological survey of a region between two great civilizations, the Sumerian of Mesopotamia and the Harappan of the Indus Valley. The vast area separating them, although virtually unexplored archeologically, nonetheless had been regarded as a cultural backwater. Since then my assistants and I have been excavating a city we found in southeastern Iran, a place called Tepe Yahya by inhabitants of villages nearby (its original name has been lost). It appears that in 4500 B.C. Tepe Yahya represented only a small village, but by 3500 B.C. it was a city of importance within the area, and by 3000 B.C. it was sharing in the international developments of the urban world of Mesopotamia.

All of the first cities discussed in this book are extinct; some are no more than dusty mounds surrounded by arid wastes. However, from what we have learned about Tepe Yahya and other ancient cities, it is evident that many of the differences between them and later urban centers are quantitative rather than qualitative. No matter what the degree of their social, economic and political complexity, all were—or are—supported to varying degrees by a surrounding network of settlements. For, once men settled down in environments of their own making they no longer could live from nature alone, but had to depend on the fruits of others' labors. This is as true for the city of Jericho in the Eighth Millennium B.C. as for Rome or New York today.

C. C. Lamberg-Karlovsky
Harvard University

Chapter One: Birth of a New Life Style

For better or for worse, the mode and manner of living that the world calls civilized began when human beings abandoned the free and easy life of hunters and food gatherers to snuggle together in settled communities. To the natural kin-cluster of family and tribe were thus added those classic symbols of fun and fury, "the neighbors." As neighbors accumulated in larger and larger numbers, villages became towns, cities, city-states and empires.

What forced this drastic turn in human affairs is only now being discovered as comfortable old theories are overturned. It is already clear that these developments proceeded with startling rapidity. Yet

The oldest city plan known, this 1500 B.C. baked-clay tablet identifies in cuneiform some of the sights of Nippur, which arose in Sumer about 5,000 years ago. Numbered on the outline drawing of the tablet are: (1) the Ekur, Sumer's most prominent religious shrine, which was dedicated to the city's chief deity, the air god Enlil; (2) the Kirishauru, the largest park in Nippur; (3) the Idshauru, Nippur's principal canal; and (4) the all-important Euphrates River.

they are astonishingly ancient. The oldest city excavated so far was established sometime around 8000 B.C.; no one doubts that still older ones wait to be uncovered. Within a few millennia, by 3500 B.C., cities were tightly organized, well governed and sophisticated, and by 2500 B.C. metropolises with the comforts and complexity of modern urban centers were in existence. The city sprang into prominence so quickly and so fully realized because it was so suited to human needs. It hastened and crystallized the evolution of social characteristics that in their crudest form, one and a half million years earlier, had given the Australopithecines an edge over the other animals of the world.

One advantage of the city was simply personal safety. One band of nomads might easily be destroyed by another, and a small settlement—simply because it was a tempting, stationary target—was even more vulnerable. But a city of several thousand souls was almost impregnable to random forays and could withstand any but the most powerful, purposeful enemy. Even natural disasters such as floods and famine were less likely to overwhelm a city, protected by its manifold resources, than they were to wipe out a village or isolated band.

Perhaps more important in the long run than personal safety was the city's promise of personal fulfillment. A variety of roles awaited the man—and woman—of the city. The city, in fact, depended on variety. Its concentration of numbers was possible only because its residents performed specialized duties that would be supported by the larger society of which the city was a part. But the possibility of specialized occupations, in turn, made the city attractive. No longer was every man forced to be a hunter or a farmer, every woman a mother and housekeeper. In the city—from the time of the very first cities—there were trade goods to be manufactured, commerce to be conducted, shrines to be tended, massive construction projects to be undertaken. The tantalizing variety of city life, offering the possibility of following a personal bent rather than a parent's footsteps, must have been as powerful a lure in 8000 B.C. as in the 20th Century A.D.

If the invention of the city seemed to fill ancient human needs, completing many aspects of social evolution that had begun much earlier, it also triggered further evolution. The city, to control its own inhabitants and also the surrounding people who provided its food, had to invent government and a legal system. It had to develop methods for organizing huge cooperative projects—training defense troops, storing grain, building city walls and eventually irrigation networks. Finally, it was to produce writing, literature and the intellectual achievements that have come to mean civilization.

Even the words city and civilization derive from the same roots, the best known and most recent of which is the medieval Latin *civis*. Yet the two concepts have been linked much longer than that, and other root words are more evocative than *civis*. A 20th Century city dweller, sprinting to catch the 5:02, may be entitled to amazement that another of the root words for city comes from the Greek word *keitai*, he lies down, or is recumbent.

Until recently, scholars thought men began to lie down in cities at the time the first powerful city-states were founded, between 3500 and 2500 B.C., in the valleys of the great rivers of antiquity: the Tigris and Euphrates in today's Iraq, the Nile in Egypt, the Indus on the Indian subcontinent. These regions still qualify as the seats of very early and impressive civilizations. But they did not contain the very first cities. In fact, since World War II almost everything assumed about "the dawn of civilization" and the origin of cities has been either turned upside down or rendered hopelessly out of date.

The refinement of scientific dating systems, such as those that measure the age of ancient relics by the radioactivity of carbon in charcoal or from the glow emitted by heated pottery, has taken much of the imaginative guesswork out of prehistoric chronology. It is these methods, plus an explosion of archeological exploration into the less accessible regions of the earth, that have pushed back the dates for the birth of cities more than 4,000 years, to about 8000 B.C. Similarly, new techniques and explorations have expanded the geographical locale of the first cities by thousands of miles. And they have also provided strikingly new insights into the social forces that brought cities into being.

But perhaps more important, this new work has demolished once and for all the old idea that cities and civilizations arose in one small corner of the world and then spread. It is clear—such romantic adventures as the voyages of *Kon-Tiki* and *Ra* to the contrary notwithstanding—that both the idea of cities and their underpinnings of agriculture, architecture, religion and social organization were invented over and over again, at different periods of time and in different configurations, all over the globe.

Today the study of man's urbanization is one of the liveliest of scholarly battlefields, an arena of intellectual brinkmanship. Onto it venture wave upon wave of learned ladies and gentlemen, announcing each new find with a glee that they mask behind esoteric reports about pottery types, animal bones, burial habits and the presence (or absence) of grain seeds and volcanic minerals. After the announcement of each new find, the scholars tend to retire to ponder their evidence and write books and, incidentally, to avoid the cross fire of other learned ladies and gentlemen who delight in taking issue with them.

Among the many questions over which modern scholars argue is an absurdly fundamental one: What, exactly, is meant by the word "city," as distinct from village, town, community or settled place?

So elusive is any precise definition that two of the world's eminent urban experts, Jacqueline Beaujeu-Garnier and Georges Chabot of France, recently threw up their scholarly hands and abandoned their scholarly syntax and said firmly that a city "is when people feel themselves to be in one."

Perhaps only common sense can define the thing. Sheer permanence of residence is one solid, agreed-upon criterion. So, in some degree, is size—both of population and of area occupied—which can be judged from the number of graves in the local cemetery, if any, the density of the houses and the limits of the city's ruins. By these criteria it is possible to define a city as a permanently inhabited place whose residents form a group larger than a family or a clan. It is also a place where there are both opportunity and demand for a division of labor, which creates social classes that recognize a differentiation in function, privilege and responsibility. The size and specialization are both cause and result of the unique role the city plays in the region. It must perform services important to the lives of those who live in and around it or travel to it. These services may be religious, administrative, commercial, political, defensive, or may involve the maintenance of water or food supplies. But whatever their form, the services must be in such demand that they give the city control over the surrounding area—on which it must depend for food to support its concentrated population.

All of these factors, evident in the cities of today, were present in ancient times—except that then no patterns had been set. No two first cities were exactly alike. They developed from local peculiarities of position or resources, and although some of them are still mysterious, still unexplained, seeming accidents or anomalies in the forward march of men, much can now be said about how this crucial invention of mankind, the city, came into being.

Because all of the first cities grew and flourished before the invention of writing in about 3500 B.C., the reasons for their existence must be deduced from scraps of archeological evidence. Almost from the birth of archeology, the accepted theory was that men settled down just as soon as they had figured out how to domesticate plants and animals. If a man could plant, control and improve the source of edible grains instead of roaming far and wide to gather them, if he could breed animals in captivity and slaughter them at will instead of chasing them across hill and dale, everything would be much more convenient. Furthermore, domestication of plants and animals combined with a sedentary life had advantages beyond convenience. These developments made both female and child labor more productive. By providing food in one place, they also permitted the survival of the weak—the young, old and sick—who might otherwise have died on the march.

Once this "food-producing revolution" had been

Black Sea

Caspian Sea

TURKEY

• Ankara   ▲ Hattusas

▲ Hacilar

▲ Catal Hüyük

▲ Çayönü

▲ Shanidar
▲ Tepe Gawra
• Erbil

▲ Tell Halaf

▲ Tell Mureybit

▲ Jarmo

CYPRUS

▲ Khirokitia

IRAQ

▲ Ganj-Dareh

Mediterranean Sea

▲ Mari

LEBANON   SYRIA

• Damascus

Euphrates R.

• Baghdad

Tigris R.

Jordan R.

▲ Jericho

Dead Sea

ISRAEL   JORDAN

▲ Nippur
Umma ▲
▲ Lagash

• Susa

▲ Uruk

Tell al-'Ubaid ▲ ▲ Ur
▲ Eridu

▲ Beidha

• Cairo

El Faiyum ▲

SAUDI ARABIA

EGYPT

Nile R.

Red Sea

The sites of 31 cities and towns that flourished
between 8000 B.C. and 1500 B.C. are spread across
a map that extends from the eastern Mediterranean
to India. Some sections of the land that are now
arid and barren were once green and productive.

■ Fertile Land   ▲ Ancient Urban Sites

□ Arid Land   ● Modern Cities

U.S.S.R.

heran

IRAN

Persian Gulf

AFGHANISTAN

▲ Shahr-I-Sokhta

▲ Tepe Yahya

PAKISTAN

Indus R.

▲ Moenjo-Daro

▲ Bala Kot

▲ Sotka-Koh
▲ Sutkagen-Dor

● Karachi

Arabian Sea

▲ Harappa

INDIA

Lothal ▲

accomplished, the old reasoning went, the relative reliability of food supply and the sedentary life increased the life span of child-bearing females, and made larger families—which made larger villages, which made increased complexity of organization and control, which made intensive agriculture necessary. Intensive agriculture demanded irrigation, scholars maintained, and that demanded organization, and then writing. The result was commerce, music, mathematics, architecture, kings, priests, empires—all centered in cities.

This chain of developing civilization was supposed to have taken place first between the Tigris and the Euphrates rivers in what is today Iraq, and then spread to the rest of the world—because that was where the oldest examples of cities, writing, organized agriculture and empires had been found combined. It was a nice, neat, logical theory, and its only defect was that it was not correct.

Today it seems strange that archeologists, anthropologists, historians and other scholars clung so long to the "food-producing revolution" as an absolute prerequisite for the establishment of urban life.

The answer lies in some peculiarities of archeology as a profession. Traditionally archeologists have depended upon museums or wealthy collectors for the funds that have enabled them to go off and search for the past. Sponsors made it quite clear that they wanted something specific and concrete in return for their support—a beautiful statue, some painted vases, a carefully worked bronze—that they could display in their showcases or in their homes. The search for the past originated as a treasure hunt, and it remained that way for years.

The first targets of the diggers were the storied cities of ancient literature or of the Bible—Homer's Troy, the Bible's Jericho, Babylon, Nineveh—or else those cities so monumental and enduring that time had not buried them, such as Athens and Rome or Memphis and Karnak in Egypt.

When such far-older sites as the cities of Sumer in Mesopotamia were found, their antiquity was overwhelming, and it seemed that here was the origin of civilization, on the banks of the mighty rivers mentioned in the Bible. ("A river flowed out of Eden to water the garden, and there it divided and became four rivers. The name of . . . the third river is Tigris, which flows east of Assyria. And the fourth river is the Euphrates.")

Yet there was a built-in trap. All of these great sites and cities, even the ones in Sumer, had flourished after the invention of writing. They assumed enormous importance because they left written records and their stories could be read.

They also left treasure troves in tomb and palace. Their remains created great museums, large private collections and beautiful art books, but they did not reveal a great deal about the origins of the civilizations to which they belonged.

Excavators often tossed away fragmented or illegible bits of inscription, tons of "ordinary" broken clay pots. No digger could be bothered, until fairly recently, to carry home animal bones and plant remains —much less lumps of desiccated human or animal excreta, tactfully called coprolites—from which subsistence patterns can be deduced.

There had been some rattlings of the scholarly applecart in the 1930s and 1940s, but the cart did not really overturn until after World War II, when archeologists armed with new ideas and new research tools descended on ancient sites from the Mediter-ranean to India, from the Himalayas to the Arabian Desert. The first jolt of discovery came from Robert J. Braidwood of the University of Chicago, who proved that agriculture did not originate in the sto-ried river valleys but in the hills above them. Later discoveries showed that agriculture, wherever it de-veloped, did not lead in a straightforward progression to villages, a settled life, cities and all their achieve-ments—pottery, weaving, trade, metallurgy, then law and religious and civic organization. A site in Syria, Tell Mureybit, revealed 17 levels of stone houses —clearly a permanently settled place. It was estab-lished in 8000 B.C. and its residents were not even farmers. Only wild grain was known to them, and all the animal bones they left behind were those of wild game taken on hunting expeditions. At a place called Shanidar, in Iraq, the intentional use of metal was raised to an art by 9000 B.C., before its practitioners had any domesticated plants.

However, the most important finds were very an-cient settlements that had not been villages but cities. Jericho disgorged the remains of a city whose inhab-itants had barely begun to domesticate grains but had the civic organization to construct a massive defen-sive wall. Catal Hüyük, a large site discovered in central Turkey, turned out to have had pottery by 6500 B.C. and also a stunningly elaborate set of re-ligious shrines—achievements characteristic of a well-developed, settled way of life—at about the same time that it first began to domesticate cattle.

For years, archeologists had connected three vari-able things: agriculture, sedentary life and cities. They had always viewed the three variables as if they were strands of a single ball of yarn, all of them tan-gled up together and rolling wildly downhill in the di-rection of urban civilization.

Once they began to untangle the strands, it was clear that there had never been one single ball of yarn. Food, obviously, was necessary for any pop-ulation to survive at all. But food in the form of agricultural production does not require a town or even a village. The farmer often lives on the land he tends instead of living in town and traveling daily to his fields. Likewise, sedentary life does not neces-sarily require agriculture: in an ecological niche of high natural production, a family can settle there and feed themselves just by gathering, as if they lived in the Garden of Eden. Nor does a city have to grow from a predecessor village of farmers or gatherers; it can be established as a city from the very beginning and can survive by trading natural resources or ser-vices considered valuable enough to be bought by their seekers in exchange for food.

Proof of the true separation of farming from per-manent settlement—and from the establishment of cities—exists all over the Near East and in Latin America, Southeast Asia and China. In Mexico, for instance, prehistoric peoples domesticated at least 10 types of food plants, including maize, by about 5000 B.C. and yet never settled into towns. They kept right on refining the agricultural process, and being semi-nomads, for another 3,500 years. Similarly, in the areas that are now Thailand, Vietnam and China, there were people who had domesticated both plants and animals and had invented pottery by the Fifth Millennium B.C., and yet who seem not to have made cities or fortifications until about 2000 B.C.

But if agriculture itself was not the key to the rise of cities, what was?

Intercity Trading in Obsidian

Obsidian, a black or gray volcanic glass that can be hewn into razor-sharp tools or delicate ritual objects, was one of the most prized materials traded among the far-flung towns of the prehistoric Near East.

City dwellers living near obsidian-producing volcanoes probably stockpiled it to pay for farm produce. In turn, farmers exchanged it with each other for goods—and so obsidian moved far from its sources.

The ancient trade routes can now be determined by a method called spectrography, which reveals distinctive traits of the material. It traces obsidian objects to the very volcanoes from which the raw material came.

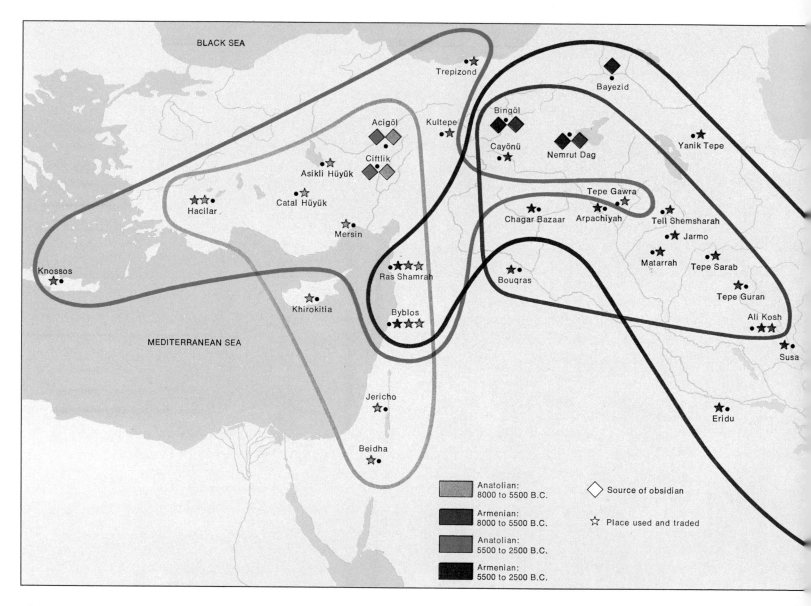

The distances over which obsidian was traded are indicated by loops on the map. Each loop is colored to match sources (diamonds) of obsidian and sites (stars) where objects made of obsidian from those sources have turned up. The loops are also keyed to successive periods to show how trade spread from two areas, called the Anatolian and Armenian.

The practical and decorative uses of obsidian in the ancient
world are demonstrated by the three objects below. The leaf-
shaped dagger was uncovered at Catal Hüyük, a city in Turkey
100 miles from a rich obsidian source; a ritual vessel sculpted
into the form of a conch shell, found on Crete, was made
of obsidian from a neighboring island; the bowl, unearthed at
Tepe Gawra, a small city in northern Iraq, was fashioned out
of a mottled chunk that came from a source 400 miles away.

CASPIAN SEA

Tal-I-Bakun

PERSIAN GULF

Bahrein

The answer is as many-sided as the character of a city itself, that most intricate of human containers. One powerful stimulus must have been sheer pressure of population. By 8000 B.C. the lingering effects of the last ice age had disappeared, and the climate had stabilized in the Near East. The ecological balance—wild grasses, wild animals, fish in the streams and fruit in the trees—was fixed and convenient for man. For the hunting and gathering people of the Near East and its environs life was easy. Their numbers increased. Then gradually it became clear that there was nowhere else to go: if a family, or a tribe, grew so numerous that its lands and game could no longer provide adequate food, the choice was either to fight the neighbors or to join them. All the territory was occupied, lightly but permanently.

One solution was to congregate, to form a cluster in some particularly fertile niche. There were places where land and climate favored intensive food gathering or food production, and the surplus people naturally went to such places.

As the population continued to expand, there was a second squeeze. When the best areas were taken, settlements appeared in less-favored regions nearby. But here small independent villages could not necessarily survive. Food was not so easy to come by, and the second-generation communities had to support themselves by providing special services—irrigation for intensive agriculture, defense, commerce, religion. But these services required large numbers of people—the beginnings of a city.

People living in a settled concentration had to defend themselves to a degree unknown to nomads—if the townsmen ran they might be able to save their lives, but they risked losing their livelihoods. This

Ruins of 6500 B.C. shops at Beidha (top), a prehistoric town in Jordan, and a 5800 B.C. bakery with round ovens at Catal Hüyük, a city in Turkey, show how specialized services sprang up to meet demands of people leading a settled life. Beidha's shops yielded animal bones, tools and beads, suggesting that butchers, toolmakers and beadmakers had worked there. Catal Hüyük's ovens, five feet across, are too large for family use and must have served the community.

need for security favored the growth of bigger settlements and even the establishment of stronghold cities in which neighboring villagers could find safety during an attack.

Once defense and population concentration had come along, there was an urgent need for control —somebody to run the city, to make decisions. A barely perceptible ruling class grew and accreted to itself the powers and prerogatives of control. Priests and shrines multiplied. If the shrines of one city seemed efficacious, they attracted worshipers from other places far away.

All these new needs—concentrated food production, defense, religion—impelled men and women to cluster in larger and larger groups. But one of the most important factors was trade. In the first cities there was no money. There were no records of transactions. Yet goods were exchanged. Primitive trade routes seem to have existed long before the first cities, but an expansion of commerce around 8000 B.C. apparently helped to account for the sudden flowering of early cities.

In some places sources of basic supply created markets: Beidha, in Jordan, had salt and natural supplies of hematite, an iron ore that then was used as a source of red coloring for pottery and rouge for women. Jericho had salt and minerals from the Dead Sea, and it was (and is) a vital stop on a main trade route —the only oasis for many miles in a dangerous desert. Catal Hüyük, in Turkey, lay near the sources of obsidian, a volcanic glass much prized in the ancient world for mirrors, knife blades, spearheads and beads. Recently discovered sites in Iran and in south-central Russia had easily worked soapstone, lapis lazuli, copper and carnelian.

These raw materials were in demand, as were the finished products of expert workmen. For years archeologists believed that trade followed cities, as cities followed agriculture. But now it is obvious that some cities grew on trade.

One of the most evocative views of the role of trade in the foundation of cities was presented by Jane Jacobs in her book *The Economy of Cities.* Jacobs posed the idea that intensive agriculture was the result, rather than the cause, of cities. Farming developed, she suggested, because large numbers of people accumulated in settled places and had to be fed. They had something to exchange for the food they wanted, and the surrounding population was willing to give up food to supply that commodity.

Jacobs invented a city that she named New Obsidian, and she located it on the Anatolian Plateau of today's Turkey, near the site of the real prehistoric city of Catal Hüyük. There on the plain, in her imaginative reconstruction, some canny types had settled close to the source of a much-prized product, obsidian. These people mined the mountains for it, hauled it home and then exchanged it for food. Some of them worked the obsidian into finished products, but others just exchanged the unworked chunks for whatever they needed.

Within her own hypothesis, Jacobs even envisioned a beguiling beginning for the whole process of domestication inside the existing city. When outlanders brought grain or animals into town to exchange them for obsidian, the locals had perforce to store these food resources. If some grains fell on the soil and grew vigorously, if some animals proved more amenable than others to captivity and to breeding in the new atmosphere, it would not have taken much wit for the city folk to notice which did what.

While Jacobs' theories are not entirely accepted, her idea of trade as a crucial factor in the rise of the first cities has been supported in general, if not in detail. Mute signs of some kind of exchange have been lurking in the ruins all the time. The cities of Mesopotamia, such as Uruk, Ur and Eridu, had no local sources of soapstone, lapis lazuli or copper. Jericho had no local source of obsidian. Catal had no sea shells or flint nearby. Yet all these foreign items turned up in the ruins of these cities. Somebody had to have brought them there, and they must have brought them for a purpose.

It is now possible to tell where many of these things came from, and thus to trace the trade routes of antiquity. In the late 1960s, a group of English scholars devised a way of identifying bits of the ubiquitous obsidian by analyzing their chemical components and relating them to known sources.

When the results were plotted on a map, there were surprises. Obsidian turns up in almost all of the traces of ancient cities, in a generally declining scale of miles from its source, but some bits that appeared in the ruins of the former Hittite capital city of Hat-

tusas, in northern Turkey, turned out not to have come from the local volcanic areas a mere 20 miles to the south but instead from today's Ethiopia, a good 2,500 miles away.

Cities across the expanse of Iran are now known to have served as trading centers for goods coming from east and west, from Sumer to the Indus Valley. There was little reason for their existence except as places where other persons could come to exchange what they had for what they would like to have.

Along the same vanished trade routes traveled an exchange of ideas, a traffic far more difficult to put into concrete terms. The men and women who walked, or sailed, or maybe even rode oxen, carried not just bags of valued goods but also ideas about gods, rulers, techniques, skills, dreams. Everywhere they went, they carried the inexplicable, exhilarating sense of a wider world.

In their exchange they helped to make not only the cities but also the city dwellers—the curious, questioning, cynical and dreaming, compromising and striving, maligned and admired ordinary people who lived in all the cities of olden times and live in all the cities of today.

Tepe Yahya— A "New" Prehistoric City

The mound of Tepe Yahya, rising from the Iranian Desert, has in one flank a 12-by-18-yard trench dug in the first probe of the site.

The term "dig" for an archeological excavation may conjure up an image of workers shoveling holes in the ground. In fact, a dig is hardly that. The meticulous work at Tepe Yahya, a 60-foot mound in southeast Iran that until 1967 concealed a prehistoric city, is a perfect example of what a delicate operation a dig really is. And it shows how much information about prehistory comes to light.

A team of archeologists, scientists, historians and artists convened each summer at Tepe Yahya to study every aspect of the ancient city as its ruins emerged. A metallurgist analyzed any metal found; a pottery expert studied the countless shards; an artist and a photographer recorded each minute detail of the project. Meanwhile, under the team's director, Iranian hands did the actual digging on a 12-yard-wide trench that was planned to cut through the mound from the top down to virgin soil. As the trench grew deeper, successive layers of the prehistoric city were laid bare.

22

An alidade—a surveyor's sighting instrument essential to archeology —helps the dig's director plot the outline of a trench to be excavated. A colleague anchors a string that is stretched to the designated spot.

Mud-brick walls demark the rooms of a house that was apparently demolished by fire 4,800 years ago. The pear-shaped trough may have been the base of an oven that was used for firing pottery or for baking bread, or both.

Steps dug into the mound reveal houses built one atop the other over a 5,000-year period. This trenching technique gives a cross section of the past, exposing finds in chronological order—the latest at the top, the oldest at the bottom.

An English specialist in Islamic pottery, Andrew Williamson, draws a cache of more than 100 vessels lying exactly as found. The ware has been meticulously brushed off but not washed or moved. Once the drawings were completed, the pots could be removed and individually scrutinized.

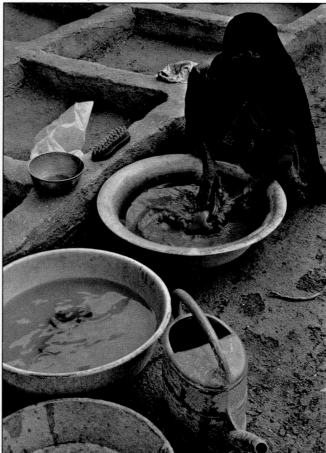

Wearing a traditional Muslim veil, a woman worker scrubs the thousands of shards that were dug up. After drying in the mud-and-straw bins behind her, the most interesting ones could be taken out for study.

A puzzle to the archeologists, this jumble of tiny doorless rooms—the largest of the rooms is hardly five feet square—was tentatively identified as the storage cellar of a 6,500-year-old house. To preserve the find during the winter months, when digging at the site was interrupted, the archeologists packed its walls with mud plaster that saves it from damage by wind, rain and snow.

Showing an enormous cut by the end
of the 1971 digging season, Tepe Yahya
towers over houses and a building
erected to store equipment. During the
winter, the Iranian government posted
two soldiers here to guard the site.

With triumphant smiles, the
archeological team and the Iranian
work crew assemble for a group
portrait over one of their most
important finds: a prosperous family's
house that yielded several foreign
seals—evidence of widespread trade.

The director of the dig, C. C. Lamberg-
Karlovsky, and his wife, Martha,
give their sons, Christopher and Karl, a
camel-back ride. The camels—owned
and rented out by one of the workers—
were used to haul wood for cooking.

Photographed from the mound, the village of Baghin, home for many of the workers, is dwarfed by the treeless Ashin Mountains. Other workers were nomadic sheep- and goatherders who camped in tents close by.

Time Off at the Dig

The dig followed an arduous routine —shoveling dirt, brushing dust off artifacts and poring over finds—but it had its light side too. Payday (below) was always welcome, and Friday was the day off for all; some took a picnic to a nearby stream or to a holy man's shrine. The less venturesome escaped the heat—110° at noon—either in the archeologists' compound or in the village (right). At sunset, though, the temperature plummeted to 50°, which was perfect for outdoor socializing and for more boisterous merrymaking (opposite, bottom).

Payday, scheduled once every 10 days, brings the workers into the courtyard of the archeologists' living compound. The dig's director (in tee shirt) doles out wages according to each worker's skill and length of service with the dig.

The women at the dig meet for tea in the courtyard of the archeologists' compound, the floor of which is covered with rugs purchased from local weavers. Such parties were a monthly event and children, too, were welcome.

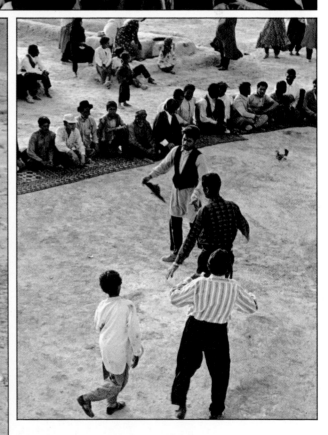

Celebrating the closing of a season's dig, Iranian workers break into a traditional all-male handkerchief dance. Later, as a regular part of the annual summer's-end festivities, barbecued sheep and goat were eaten.

Chapter Two: The Walls of Jericho

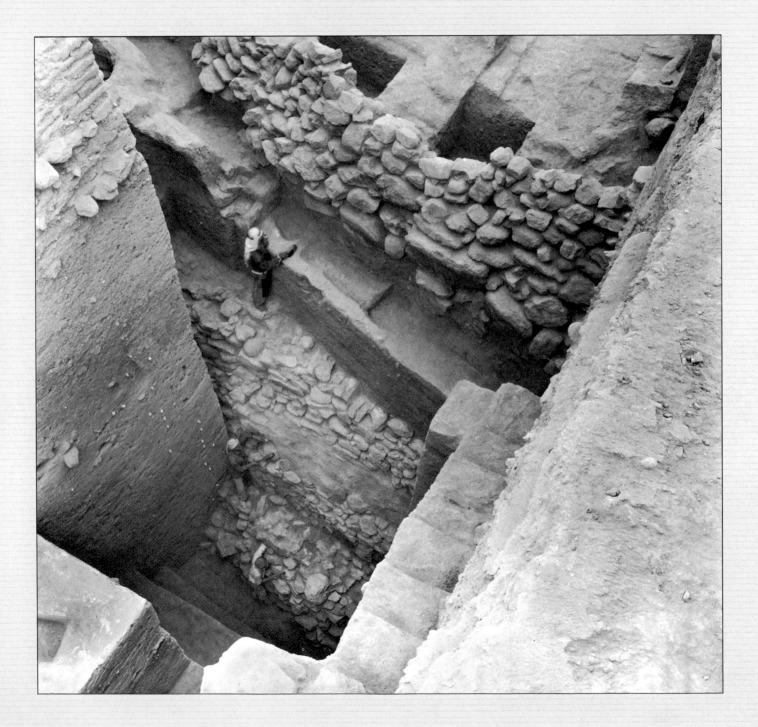

When it is approached by air, Jericho stands out as a tiny green oasis set in a glittering expanse of desert. The modern city is a cluster of lush parks, palm trees and attractive homes. The city was built mainly by rich Arabs, but it has since been absorbed by Israel in the Six-Day War of 1967. Just north of the modern city is a bulging mound, which is of far greater significance to archeologists than the present Jericho. They have carved up the mound into a network of trenches to study the layers of civilization below the surface; for beneath this now-welted and pock-marked ground lies the evidence of a much earlier Jericho, and in fact the oldest city yet to be discovered anywhere in the world.

This ancient Jericho was inhabited, over a period that lasted more than 65 centuries, by at least 10 different cultures. At different times its different inhabitants built various kinds of houses, a tower and that public work for which Jericho is famous: a wall.

One of the undisputed criteria for achieving the title of "city" is a community's ability to embark upon public works: to build a temple, a canal, a monument, a wall. Hunters, nomads, prehistoric villagers devoted all their energies and their expanding knowledge to their own survival. They never had enough hands or resources to engage upon public works. Nor had they worked out a division of labor to enable them to do so. Even had some adventurous food-gatherer con-

Although the Biblical wall that fell flat to the sound of Joshua's trumpets has never been found, excavations at Jericho have uncovered other, far more ancient walls. The two oldest are shown here: The rough wall looming over the Arab worker's head, about six feet high, was built of large stones about 6000 B.C., while the wall on which he stands, made of smaller stones and 20 feet high, was put up about 8000 B.C. and may have been the first city wall ever erected.

ceived the idea of building a wall, who would have provided him with food and shelter while he worked at his folly? Public works, with a few exceptions, have been undertaken only by large and complex communities. Indeed, it was the discovery of the great ziggurats of Sumer and the mighty pyramids of Egypt that led archeologists to decide that the world's first cities had arisen in the famous fertile crescent in the Fourth Millennium B.C.

Then in the 1950s came new discoveries about Jericho and its walls, and archeologists had to alter their assumptions. Jericho proved to be so old that it was ancient when the pyramids were new; and the walls of Jericho represent a public work on a scale that presupposes community cooperation and division of labor. Jericho had many walls, built and rebuilt at different times, some on the remains of old ones, some on different limits of the city. Some were razed by invaders; some fell in earthquakes; some simply eroded in the sun, the rain and the wind when the city was abandoned, as it was from time to time over its long history. But the oldest wall that man has found dates from a near-incredible 8000 B.C.—5,000 years before Egypt's pyramids and Sumer's temples. Furthermore, this oldest public work yet discovered was no sometime boundary of piled-up pebbles. It was a solid, free-standing structure built of boulders that had to be dragged in from outside the town and set in place without benefit of mortar. It is six feet six inches thick at its base. How tall it was originally nobody knows; but the tallest remaining section, after 10,000 years of destruction and erosion, stands a full 12 feet, well over twice the height of the average man of the Ninth Millennium B.C.

The fact that there was a Jericho and that it had a

wall did not come as a surprise to modern man. Most people had read all about it in the Old Testament. And anyone who had missed that account had heard the stirring strains of "Joshua fit the battle of Jericho . . . and the walls came tumbling down." The surprise came when the wall was dated by modern scientific techniques. Joshua had led the Israelites into Palestine about 1500 B.C. This wall proves to have been built more than 6,000 years before Joshua's miraculous accomplishment.

It was, in fact, Joshua who first led the archeologists to Jericho. The year was 1867 and the sponsors were the Palestine Exploration Fund, the first body in Great Britain (and one of the first in the world) to engage in archeological research. It was an era of anxious debate between the traditional religious concepts of human development and the evolution theory of Charles Darwin. The purpose of the Palestine Exploration Fund—to which Darwin himself made a contribution of eight guineas—was to make a scientific study of the land of the Bible; and the obliging British government dispatched a crew of welltrained men of the Royal Engineers to the Holy Land to aid in digging up the evidence.

In Jericho the engineers found the hill that 10,000 years of occupation, abandonment and weathering had made of the ancient city. They started digging at the south end. At 10 feet they found nothing more interesting than some charred wood, the significance of which escaped them. At 20 feet they gave up. They had in fact arrived at about the middle of an enormous wall of the Early Bronze Age, circa 3000 B.C., but they did not recognize it as a wall.

Perhaps it is just as well that they did not. For this structure was 1,500 years older than the one Joshua

Who—or what—destroyed ancient Jericho? This 15th Century German woodcut shows Joshua's priests tumbling the walls with trumpet blasts. But archeological evidence suggests that Jericho may have been destroyed instead by an earthquake—and not once, apparently, but several times.

was supposed to have blown down; and it is easy to imagine the tumult that would have been caused in pious breasts in Britain if any evidence had disproved the Bible's story.

Forty years later an Austro-German expedition went to Jericho and dug between 1908 and 1911. These excavators found some pottery fragments, but not the easily dated inscriptions or coins they had hoped for, and they did not realize the great age of the pottery they had found. So, like the British group that had preceded them, the Austro-German team abandoned the project and came away with nothing startling to report.

The man who first sounded the alarm that Jericho was going to upset the scholarly and Biblical time-tables was the late John Garstang, who was a professor of archeology at Liverpool University. Digging from 1930 to 1935, he found a double wall, and tentatively ascribed it to the time of Joshua. (The date later turned out to be in error; the wall was in fact much older.) Digging deeper, Garstang made the puzzling discovery that all the lower levels of the mound —the levels occupied by the earliest settlers of Jericho—had no pottery.

Here was a dilemma. Archeologists had for years thought that pottery went along with the earliest villages and towns, that it was a creation of the first human groups who gave up the nomadic life and settled down. Yet here in Jericho was evidence of a large, permanent community that had flourished for centuries before it had pottery.

This particular mystery was not solved in Jericho but in other early cities, where it was found that pottery was not always present. But it was the puzzle of the missing pottery that led to the most astonishing discoveries in Jericho. Britain's Dame Kathleen Kenyon, then Director of the British School of Archaeology at Jerusalem, went to Jericho in 1952 to see if she could find any pottery, or some reason for its absence. And it is with her that the latter-day saga of the ancient city begins.

In her first digging season Kenyon found a wall of unexpected antiquity: it dated all the way back to 6000 B.C. Kenyon referred to her find in scientific journals as the earliest known town wall in the world; and four years later she confessed in another scholarly article that she had used the word "known" only because she was convinced that Jericho would produce a still older one. Then, obligingly, it did: not only one, but two.

The first of these older walls Kenyon uncovered had been built in about 7000 B.C. It was constructed of large, unworked stones, free-standing on their outer edges but supported inside by a fill of rubble and rock almost 10 feet high. The wall itself must have stood, by Kenyon's estimate, more than 15 feet high. Its inner face did double service, with many houses built against it. The other wall was built about 8000 B.C. of smaller stones than the later one; but the earlier stones had been far more carefully set. In places, the wall still survived to a height of almost 20 feet, and its foundations rested firmly on bedrock that was 50 feet below the surface of the ancient mound. Outside the foundations, the prehistoric wall builders had carved out of solid rock an enormous ditch 27 feet wide and 9 feet deep. How they could have made this excavation, and at what terrible toll of labor in Jericho's withering heat, remains a puzzle. There could hardly have been more than two or three thousand inhabitants on the 10 acres that made up Jericho in 8000 B.C. But somehow among them they managed to haul a sufficient number of stones from a river bed half a mile away to build their wall, and then they managed to cut that mighty trench. Perhaps they used stone mauls. Perhaps they had figured out how to split stone by heating it with fire and then dousing it with water. No one knows.

Today the oldest wall and its ditch lie at the bottom of the excavators' trench, which is 50 feet deep. Peering down toward it is a queasy experience, like looking down a fathomless hole into the murk of the prehistoric past. But perhaps an even more remarkable discovery than the ditch itself was a solid stone tower on the inner side of the wall, a structure tall enough and massive enough to have graced one of the great medieval castles of France. The tower is more than 30 feet in diameter at the base, and even in ruins it stands 30 feet high. Carefully built into the center is a flight of steps going down to a horizontal passage at near-bedrock level. Each stair tread is a single great stone slab, hammered smooth. Similar smoothed slabs form the roof of the staircase and the passage below. Where the passage led and exactly how many steps there once were have not been determined, because the staircase now vanishes underneath a heap of 70 feet of debris left by the ancient townspeople and the modern archeologists.

At the bottom of the tower, Kenyon's excavators made another tantalizing discovery: 12 skeletons, all crammed into a narrow space. Dating shows them to be 9,000 years old. Could they have been brave defenders of Jericho, forerunners of the martyrs of the Alamo? Apparently not: because—equally mysteriously—carbon dating indicates that the tower was not being used, and was eroding away, during that period. It is possible that this was a common grave.

Around the tower and along the wall runs an example of public works a lot more puzzling than the wall or the tower. The excavators have found only the walls of these structures, walls with no opening whatever except a top channel 18 inches deep. But when found, the channels were full of silt. Silt implies running water. And running water at this height implies aqueducts, possibly for a sanitation system and possibly for a form of irrigation.

Kenyon believes that these structures may indeed have been built for purposes of irrigation. Not all archeologists agree, since 7000 B.C. is early for so sophisticated a public work. Presumably, since this oasis city has such a bountiful supply of water, the life-giving liquid was sluiced out onto the fields. But no field forms or channels survive, and whatever gardens once bloomed have now reverted to desert. In any case, if these ancients of Jericho did have a method of irrigation, as Kenyon suggested they might have had, they were engaged in a more complex form of civic organization than building a wall or even organizing a defense. The people had to calculate not only how the water was to be conveyed to the channels but also when it would be released, toward which fields it should flow and for how long. And someone, no doubt, had to arbitrate among the competing claims for water.

Water is in fact central to the history of Jericho. That history began long before the rise of the city, about two million years ago, when a gigantic shudder ruffled the earth's surface in the eastern Mediterranean and a big slice of the outer crust dropped half a mile vertically. The trough this cataclysm formed begins in Syria, runs down through Israel

An aerial view of the town of Erbil (top), in Iraq, presents the appearance the site of Jericho (above) might have had. The rise on which Erbil stands, like the mound that is all that remains of ancient Jericho, is composed of ruins of successive settlements—but Jericho's mound is older and taller.

(where it varies from five to 12 miles wide), becomes the Gulf of Aqaba, part of the Red Sea, and then the Great Rift Valley of Eastern Africa. The River Jordan, which rises in the Lebanese mountains, flows through this trough to the Biblical Sea of Galilee, today called the Lake of Tiberias, and finally ends in the Dead Sea at 1,300 feet below sea level.

Jericho lies on a flat plain between these two seas and two mountain ranges. The city is nearly 1,000 feet below sea level, which makes it extraordinarily hot, and the intense desert heat burns the surrounding area white, except for a few weeks in the spring. But not Jericho. From deep underneath the earth's surface a welling spring has provided an oasis at this spot since the earliest times. Today the water still rushes up, at the generous rate of about a thousand gallons a minute; but now of course it pours into a modern concrete-walled reservoir.

This inexhaustible water supply, gushing up in the midst of the desert, has nourished the peoples of Jericho since the Ninth Millennium B.C.; and there are traces of visitors, and fairly regular visitors at that, as early as 9500 B.C. These early people were the Natufians, a cave-dwelling group that lived in the hills nearby; they had sickles, pounders and a type of stone for grinding wild grains. And their concerns went beyond the utilitarian; at Jericho they left a mysterious structure that may have been a shrine. As it stands today it is primarily an oval platform of clay, buttressed with stones; its walls have two socket stones that may have supported something like totem poles. In the nearby debris was found one bone harpoon head, which links the Natufians with other peoples in the region.

Little more is known about these dimly seen early

An aerial view of Jericho encompasses the modern city and the 50-foot-high dirt mound under which lie buried the many cities and walls of ancient Jericho. The most recent excavation can be seen as the trench cutting from left at the bottom of the photograph.

settlers. They were followed by a group whom archeologists call, prosaically, Pre-Pottery Neolithic A. They inhabited Jericho at about 8000 B.C. They lived in round houses made of sun-dried mud brick, formed by hand without the aid of molds. The bricks were "hog-backed," or humped, at the top, and thus Kathleen Kenyon, the first to unearth their remains, calls the people who made them the hog-backed brick people. Although they had no pottery as such, they developed the cooperation and the division of labor to produce public works: they built a wall—and rebuilt it again and again over a period of 700 years.

They in turn were supplanted, around 7000 B.C., by a more advanced group of people who also used bricks, but of a different type—cigar-shaped and with a herringbone pattern impressed in the top by the thumbs of the brickmakers. The thumbprints served a double purpose: different numbers of thumbprints indicated the placement of each brick in the wall, and the thumbprint indentations held the mortar with which they were set. For this new breed of Jericho's inhabitants had learned how to make the important adhesive, mortar, probably by heating limestone and then mixing this "burned lime" with sand and water. They used their knowledge not only in their additions to the walls of the city. They also employed mortar to build their houses; and they used burned lime to plaster their walls and floors. They are accordingly known as the plastered-floor people. They may have come from somewhere nearby, perhaps from one of the countless undiscovered mounds in the deserts of the Near East that still await the spades of the archeologists.

Another practice that differentiates the plastered-floor people from their predecessors is the shape in which they built their houses: they were rectangular. The switch from round to rectangular dwellings is an intriguing, still mysterious step in the development of human settlement. The circle and the arc are present in nature—in the shape of a tree trunk, a cave roof, a rainbow, even the far horizon. But the rectangle is almost always made by man.

The plastered-floor people evidently got along for about 1,000 years without a new wall. By 6000 B.C. they had built another. They made it of much larger stones than its predecessor. And inside the wall they left what today's excavators regard as a grisly indication of why the new wall was built. Forty skeletons buried within the wall suggest the possibility that Jericho had to be defended against aggressors outside its ramparts.

There is, in fact, further evidence that the city was a center of attraction, because it was a center of trade. The ruins of Jericho have turned up more and more traces of foreign goods, like obsidian, sea shells and hematite, an iron-oxide mineral much prized in the ancient world for its red color. These commodities, which had to be imported, are marks of increased movement of people in the Middle East. And Jericho had items to draw travelers. It had minerals from the nearby Dead Sea, principally salt, the importance of which is easy to underestimate in the 20th Century: salt was a prized commodity in the ancient world, particularly as a preservative for food.

As early as 8500 B.C. a primitive sort of trade had arisen in the Near East—the simple exchange of one useful or prized article for another—and by 7000 B.C. Jericho was engaged in it. The city was uniquely situated and endowed to take advantage of this early trade. It lay on a natural route of the ancient world,

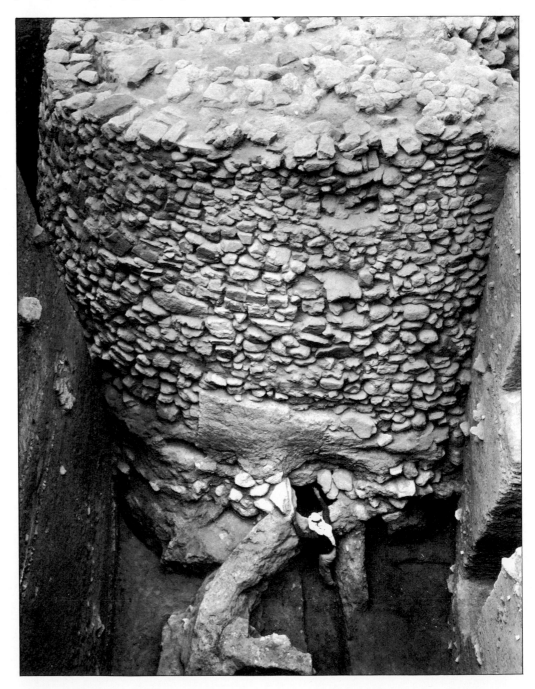

A massive stone tower, built presumably for defense around 8000 B.C., stands 30 feet high against the inside of Jericho's ancient walls. The entrance at the bottom—where a man crouches—opens onto a narrow passage leading to a flight of steps.

Digging Deep into Urban History

The oldest city yet discovered is the one that lies next to the modern town of Jericho, at a depth of 70 feet and under a mound of rocks, dust, earth and other Jerichos. This first community, on a site that has since been almost continuously inhabited, was built about 10,000 years ago.

But despite the many excavators drawn to the area over the decades, the oldest of the many Jerichos was not unearthed until Dame Kathleen Kenyon, then Director of the British School of Archaeology at Jerusalem, dug down to the earliest level in the 1950s. There she found the ruins of small round houses, a massive defense wall six feet wide and a tower 30 feet high. The houses (one is seen in the picture at bottom right on the opposite page) may duplicate the beehive shape of nomads' huts—perhaps indicating the reluctance of the settlers to abandon a shape familiar to them. But the wall and tower, built thick enough to withstand the depredations of both men and time, show that this early city, which covered about 10 acres and contained some 2,000 people, already had the sophistication and organization required for ambitious public works.

Five men mark the levels of ancient Jericho. The top figure stands on the mound's present surface, the one below on a tower built in 8000 B.C., the next two near a wall erected around the same time, and the last looks up from a ditch cut by hand from living rock.

Two distinct types of houses mark the first two occupations of Jericho. The inhabitants of 7000 B.C. built dwellings with rectangular floor plans (below), but 1,000 years earlier settlers lived in round houses, indicated by the foundation of one seen at bottom.

between the Anatolian Plain in the north, which had obsidian and greenstone, and the agricultural village of Beidha in the southeast, which had hematite and sea shells. Jericho may well have been an important stop on this very ancient trade route. The city's salt, water and food supplies might have been compelling lures to travelers.

A full-fledged city it was, then, with its public works, perhaps its legions for defense, and a center for vagabond traders. This much the unearthed remains made fairly clear. But some of the archeologists' discoveries were not so easily interpreted. The bones and skulls of some persons were preserved inside the houses—why can only be guessed at. But far more puzzling—perhaps the most startling finds of Jericho—are some strange-looking human skulls that date to about 6000 B.C.

Their discovery had a drama all its own. During Kenyon's 1953 excavation, a piece of human cranium, white and shiny, was visible throughout the summer, in one wall of a trench excavation. But Kathleen Kenyon likes straight lines; she says that "it looks most untidy to have the sides of the excavation pockmarked by pits dug into them." So she forbade anyone to remove the piece of skull. Finally, however, at the end of the season, she gave permission to remove it. When the diggers got it out they discovered, to the amazement of all on hand, that it had been fitted carefully with a plaster face and eyes made of sea shells.

Nothing like this had ever been discovered. Kenyon's archeologists excitedly dug further. Behind that first skull were two more. When these were removed, there were three more. And behind them, a seventh. The entire scientific expedition had packed up a day

or so before, intending to return home until the next digging season. But when the plastered skulls were discovered everybody decided to stay on for an extra week, eating and sleeping and sitting on a bare-earth floor, while they dug out and examined their surprising new discoveries.

Each skull had been packed carefully with clay, and each had been painstakingly rebuilt on the outside with a face that presumably resembled the one it had borne in life. For no two plastered skulls are identical. Their precise purpose is not clear, but it seems quite likely that they were kept as family portraits. In later millennia, the Romans were to commission and treasure sculptured busts of their ancestors; and even in modern times people keep family paintings of their forebears.

Sometime after 6000 B.C. Jericho was abandoned. Its people wandered away, and their walls, their tower and the bones of their ancestors were left to the drifting sand. It was perhaps 1,000 years before Jericho was inhabited again, by a new race of people. And in one of Jericho's many surprises, these new inhabitants seem to have been far less sophisticated than their predecessors. They did not build houses, but only dug rudimentary shelters. They had no recognizable graves, and must have left their dead to the elements and the animals. And they built no wall. But, in a curious exception to the archeological theory, these people, who were evidently too primitive to engage in public works, did make pottery.

With these pottery makers, who happened to be unskilled in architecture, the ancient days of Jericho could be said to end. By the time a new group of inhabitants had taken up residence in the city it was 3000 B.C. and the dawn of the Bronze Age. These

Faces from the past, these two heads are not sculptures but skulls covered with clay and given cowrie-shell eyes. They were found embedded in one of Jericho's ancient stone walls and suggest an early form of ancestor worship, perhaps one that called for the immortalization of the dead through preservation of their facial features.

city people not only preserved their dead; they buried them in tombs, thus preserving with them a wealth of information for the archeologists. The latest citizens of Jericho dug deep shafts into the limestone, and carved out underground chambers in which they placed one or more bodies together with their worldly possessions, such as beads, daggers, food or furniture. The remnants of their civilization were thus left to help modern man reconstruct their existence in Jericho 5,000 years ago.

And these people left something else: an intriguing bit of evidence that was discovered in an unexpected way. On the 1956 Kenyon dig, as on so many archeological expeditions, there never seemed to be enough ladders to put down into all the inviting nooks and crannies of excavation. From long experience many archeologists have learned to substitute a rope, held at the top of the pit by a companion while the investigator lets himself down hand over hand, his feet braced against the side of the excavation. After he has completed his study, he calls for his colleague to hold fast while he hauls himself back to the surface.

One member of the Kenyon expedition had gone down into the pit by this archeological technique, and later a sudden thunderstorm swept down on Jericho. Hearing the thunder and seeing the lightning, the explorer called for his companion to hold onto the rope so he could climb back up again. But evidently the thunderstorm had frightened his rope holder away, for he could not be found.

The stranded man shouted. He yelled. But in the thunder he could not be heard. So, with nothing else to do, he began to examine the walls of his prison.

To his astonishment he found graffiti, the scratchings of men 5,000 years his predecessors. There were

A magical symbol, or perhaps an early attempt at plane geometry, these overlapping triangles were scratched into a piece of soft limestone, measuring about two feet long, that was discovered in the debris of ancient Jericho. The enigmatic markings have been dated back some 5,000 years.

animals with long horns, which may be goats. There were trees, and two stick-figure men with shields and spears. The observer was so fascinated with his find that he was not ready to climb his rope when his colleague returned.

The graffiti discovered by accident were not very accomplished art, but they did represent a type of culture that Jericho had not produced before. And this culture may well have had a link with those that by this time had grown up to the north and south of the city. To the south there was Egypt; to the northeast there were the burgeoning cities of Mesopotamia. The route between these giants of the ancient world and their smaller contemporaries ran along the Jordan Valley rift formed by the great earthquake of two million years ago.

The Bronze Age, which lasted for some 1,500 years, was the one in which these civilizations were to flower. During this time many new peoples came and went in Jericho; and many of them built new walls. In fact they built and rebuilt walls at least 20 times between 3000 B.C. and 2300 B.C. The rebuilding implies that Jericho was frequently attacked, or at least menaced. Most of these Bronze Age walls are double, with a small space in between. The ancient engineers may have ordered the walls built this way deliberately, so that if one wall were breached by attack, by earthquake, even by old age, the parallel wall would still stand. There is evidence in the ruins that small sections did topple frequently, and that they were quickly repaired.

The remains of these Bronze Age walls are confusing for other reasons. They intersect each other, superimpose on each other, wander both inside and outside the remains of earlier walls. By now the site of Jericho was an accumulation of four or five thousand years. To add to the confusion provided by the jumble of walls, the site was alternately occupied and abandoned over this 1,500-year period; the different peoples had different practices; and when the site was abandoned the elements eroded it, wiping out many important clues in the process.

The last flicker of life in the old city came with the Biblical Battle of Jericho, which must have occurred about 1500 B.C. Whatever walls Joshua sent tumbling down have been erased by erosion. Civilization in this region went on in other cities familiar to readers of the Bible, Jerusalem and Megiddo. But Jericho, as if fulfilling Biblical prophecy, was abandoned at some time after Joshua's assault. When the oasis was put to use again in modern times, the new settlers chose a site a few yards to the south.

Today, ironically, even the spring that gave it life seems to have forsaken the confines of ancient Jericho. The spring is now separated from the mound by a road, and it bubbles out into a concrete-walled reservoir that looks like a half-empty swimming pool. Its waters are hustled without ceremony into a network of pipes that disperse it to the modern city of Jericho and to irrigation channels out of sight across the desert—no less a public work than the nearby wall built by men of 10,000 years ago.

Chapter Three: The Shrines of Catal Hüyük

Since the search for man's urban origins began in earnest after the Second World War, few sites have proved so enigmatic—or so downright fascinating —as that of a dusty, 58-foot-high mound on the banks of a stream in what is now south-central Turkey.

This area is far from the traditional cradles of civilization, and no community here was ever hinted at in any of the ancient writings. Yet the mound is there, remains of a city at least 8,500 years old. It was no mere farming village or small town; it covered 32 acres, enough to house at least 6,000 persons, the biggest site of its time yet excavated. Like Jericho, it presumably was a trading center, but it may equally have owed its existence to another function that became a hallmark of the developing cities—religious service. So many of the ancient buildings unearthed here seem to have been shrines that this great mound may cover a city that was supported as a center for sacred observances in addition to its other activities.

No one knows what the energetic residents called themselves, nor what they called their city. And in fact, only one of the 32 acres has been completely uncovered and studied. The name now given the city, Catal Hüyük (pronounced Chatal Hooyook), is modern Turkish, deriving from a fork in the road at the northern end of the city mound—"Catal" means fork and "Hüyük," mound. But of how its residents lived, much can be said. For the excavations of that one acre have revealed homes and art works as well as

A bow-carrying hunter of 6000 B.C., one of many lively figures depicted in the earliest wall painting yet discovered in the world, appears on a fragment of the so-called Hunting Shrine at Catal Hüyük, the 8,000-year-old city on the Anatolian Plain of south-central Turkey. The archer wears a spotted leopard sash that is believed to indicate his priestly status.

fragments of bone, pollen and charcoal that, when analyzed by new techniques, tell what these people wore and ate, what they looked like, even the way they buried their dead. By drawing on the minute details supplied by scientists of many disciplines, it is even possible to reconstruct the beginning of an ordinary day in Catal Hüyük 8,000 years ago.

When the first light of dawn struck this place on a spring morning in the year 6000 B.C., it brushed lightly across the flat roofs of tightly built mud-brick houses. Each was set against its neighbor as tightly and neatly as the pueblo dwellings of the American Indians in the southwestern United States. Pueblo houses often were terraced up the side of a cliff, but in Catal they rose one against another on the ruins of earlier houses, creating their own "cliff" as the habitation level rose. Even the color of Catal's walls was like that of the pueblo—the warm brown of mud. In Catal, as in many of the pueblo dwellings, the houses turned blank, doorless walls to the world. The household entrance was by way of the roof through either a wooden doorway or a thatch opening onto a ladder (pages 48-49). Doors at ground level could have let in anything from floodwaters to wild animals: the roof holes and ladders provided security.

The sun rose behind the mountains, which loomed dark blue against the light blue of the dawn sky. Two of the peaks were active volcanoes, spurting their fury into the air at intervals. A third, the one nearest town, was dormant. The sun's beams splintered behind the mountains, flying outward like volcanic particles. The solar fireworks, still visible in the 20th Century to those who live near mountains and rise early, glinted from the water of the stream and turned the fresh green of growing wheat and barley near-luminescent. Outside the town, cultivated fields stretched along the banks of the river.

No cock's crow shattered the silence of dawn, because in Catal Hüyük there were no domestic fowl. Outside, there was a faint dry sound of sharp hoofs on stream gravel, as small herds of sheep and goats went to the river to drink. Some dogs barked, for the people of Catal Hüyük did have domesticated dogs.

Inside one of the houses the father stirred. He was a relatively tall fellow, at five feet seven inches, sturdy and well-muscled, dark-haired and sun-tanned. He had slept the night on a woven mat laid on a low mud-brick platform in the northeast corner of the room. The sun woke him, striking through the small open window high up near the ceiling and lighting the rungs of the wooden ladder that led to the entrance hole in the roof. He groped across the top of his sleeping platform, searching for his tool kit. It was all in a little leather pouch that he suspended from his belt by leather thongs during the day. Inside was a lump of yellowish, crystalline sulfur collected on his last trip to the hills, and a flint tool that he had fashioned to his needs. The tool had a sharp scraper on one end, a blunt striking knob on the other and in the middle a sharp edge to serve as a cutter. With this prehistoric Boy Scout knife the man could make wood shavings, strike a spark, feed the spark with sulfur and produce a fire within minutes. He could not kill an animal with the tool, but he could scrape a skin, sharpen a digging tool and hammer at small objects.

On that morning he wore night clothes that were also his day clothes: a loose-fitting loincloth woven of some light material, probably wool. His leather sandals lay near his bed, but he got up and climbed the entrance ladder barefoot—it was a warm morning and his feet were toughened to the rungs. He blinked a bit in the morning brightness, then walked across the smooth flat roof of his own house, across that of his neighbor's, and let himself down by another ladder into a courtyard 20 feet away. This open space was in fact the ruins of a house like his own, one that had been abandoned when its owners died or moved away. Now, its roof and walls crumbled, it had become a public toilet and refuse dump for the immediate vicinity. Those who used it regularly carried there the ashes from their ovens and hearth fires, and a few handfuls of ash were sufficient to cover the accumulating refuse and to guard against both flies and stench.

When he got home, his wife and children were up. They had slept apart from him, on a large platform on the east wall of the large single room—about 18 by 20 feet in size—near the kitchen area and the warmth left by its fires. The kitchen area consisted of a round baking oven set into the south wall, and in the floor nearby a raised open hearth. The smoke from both went up through the roof entrance hole.

The man made a fire on the hearth while his wife went through a small doorless opening in the mud-brick wall to the family food-storage niche. In it was a bin about a yard high, made of clay and very clean. She drew some grain from a small hole at the bin's bottom: it was always filled from the top and emptied from the bottom so that the oldest grain, or that most exposed to damp, would be used first. The wife moved slowly. She was heavy with another child, and she was getting old: almost 28.

On that mythical morning the family ate a gruel of grain and milk, supplemented by bits of meat left over

The 32-acre, 58-foot-high mound that covers the ancient town of Catal Hüyük is outlined on this topographical map, with the numbered circles indicating the height (in feet) of the levels above the Konya Plain. The one-acre section excavated in the 1960s is indicated by the dark area. Artifacts dating from about 6500 B.C. have been unearthed at the site, and archeologists surmise that the town may date as far back as 8300 B.C. Inexplicably, it was abandoned about 5600 B.C.

from a previous meal. The mother nursed the baby while she fed the next-oldest with a spoon made from a cow's rib bone. It was a perfect implement: once gruel was fed into the wide blunt end of the bone, it slid gently down to the narrow end and then slowly, in small doses, into the small mouth.

Then there was work to do. The oldest child was dispatched to bring water from the stream for cooking and washing, and to tend to the animals kept in community pens outside the little city.

The woman set herself to making a basket of river reeds. It would hold the precious grains of wheat and barley, taken from the clay-lined storage bins in the house, which provided food for her family. The man climbed back up to his roof to examine it carefully for repair; this was an annual chore. The roof was made first of a mat of river reeds, very closely woven, which fitted over the timbers of the ceiling and kept bits of plaster from falling inside. On top of them went a layer of rough bundles of reeds, tied together and laid closely in rows. On top of the bundles were a thick mud cover and a layer of plaster made from a white clay found nearby. This roof had not only to keep out the yearly rainfall, which was only about 16 inches, but also to serve as passage to the other houses. It had to be strong, for it also functioned as street, auxiliary work space, and sometimes as a sleeping and living area during the hottest nights of the year. (Even today, in this part of Turkey, country folk use ladders to reach the flat roofs where they sleep in summer and do household chores year round.)

Spring was a busy time in Catal Hüyük. Once the rains had ended, all the structures in the little city had to be renovated, crops sown, and the complex burial rites performed. The houses had timber corner posts and cross bracings with walls made of bricks —formed in wooden molds, usually thirteen and a half by six and a half by three and a half inches, and squared with an adz. Mud is a good, easily worked building material, but it disintegrates in the dampness. So each spring, after the rains, repairs had to be made; then, in the dry summer, the bricks and the plaster with which they were covered would harden and be solid again for autumn. Inside the houses, on top of the brick, went a thin layer of plaster made of fine white clay mixed with water. (The excavators found as many as 120 coats of plaster on the walls, indicating that they were renovated again and again.) This plaster covered everything—sleeping platforms, hearth, oven, walls, ceiling, floor—and applying it all must have required an orgy of spring cleaning.

Whether the man and his wife spent their day in these spring activities can only be guessed at. They might have tended fields or flocks, but not many townsfolk could have been farmers—no compact community of 6,000 people could have grown enough food to support itself while doing all the other things that Catal Hüyük residents did. The city must have traded goods and services for supplies from the surrounding region. The woman of the house might conceivably have made baskets for such trade. Or the man might have spent his days as a craftsman, for although no specialized tools were found in his home, there is ample evidence in the city of skillfully woven textiles, good pottery and beautiful art work. Or the couple might have served in some priestly office; in the single acre uncovered at Catal Hüyük, one of every three buildings seems to have been a religious shrine.

Thus there was no scarcity of possible occupations

in Catal Hüyük; 8,000 years ago it had achieved a high degree of urbanization, with a labor force apparently grouped by specialties, an extensive traffic with the world outside, some form of civic organization to direct its diverse activities, a rich endowment of art and elaborate religious edifices.

From the beginning of the Catal Hüyük excavation in the early 1960s, the city's sophistication astonished and exasperated the experts. To a generation of archeologists schooled to believe that urban communities did not arise until the Fourth Millennium B.C., and then in Mesopotamia, Catal Hüyük seemed to be in the wrong place, at the wrong time, and the wrong size. It was also mysteriously prosperous. All these puzzles are complicated by the personality of the city's discoverer and chief biographer, James Mel-

A contemporary portrait of an early city, this painting on the wall of a shrine in Catal Hüyük shows the town's buildings rising in graded terraces against a backdrop of the erupting twin-peaked volcano Hasan Dag (dotted section at left) some 80 miles away. The mural, radiocarbon dated at about 6200 B.C., is the earliest known example of landscape art.

laart of the Institute of Archeology at the University of London. He is as enigmatic and as energetic as the citizens of Catal Hüyük themselves.

As a very young man, Mellaart developed the reputation of being a "lucky" archeologist—a reputation that may well spring from some of his stunning finds; but the fact is that he is a hard-working scholar who prepared himself well. One of his first jobs, in 1952, was as a field assistant to Kathleen Kenyon in Jericho. There he went out for a stroll one evening, noted a strange shadow on the earth, found it to be a slight depression and turned up a tomb with 40 intact pottery vases. On another day, on Cyprus, he pleaded lack of funds as a reason for not going into town with fellow archeologists on a celebration. Instead he trudged back to the site where they had been working, and found a treasure in Mycenaean bronze.

But Turkey was the land to which he was drawn, partly because it was just beginning to be explored and promised to yield rich finds. He spent two years trudging over the Anatolian Plateau with his sparse belongings in a knapsack and the pockets of his baggy trousers filled with small rocks to hurl at marauding dogs. The foreigner with the round, bespectacled face and mussed-up hair became familiar to the Turkish villagers, and as he learned their language they led him to mounds they knew about, to broken inscriptions half buried in weeds and to sites where their farm plows had turned up bits of broken pottery. In 1957 Mellaart began to dig on the Anatolian Plateau, at Hacilar, a small site about 165 yards in diameter and five and a half yards high that yielded painted pottery and architectural remains indicating that the site had been inhabited in two different and widely separated periods. One habitation was an early agricultural village dating back to about 7000 B.C.; the other, above it, and more sophisticated, dated from about 5700 B.C.

Somewhere, Mellaart thought, there must be another settlement that would fit into that gap of 1,300 years. He remembered having seen, years before, far off against the sky near Konya, a strange and enormous mound. In 1958, with two companions, he set out to investigate it.

Much of the mound "was covered by turf and ruinweed," Mellaart wrote later, "but where the prevailing southwesterly winds had scoured its surface bare there were unmistakable traces of mudbrick buildings, burned red in a conflagration contrasting with patches of gray ash, broken bones, potsherds and obsidian tools and weapons. To our surprise these were found not only at the bottom of the mound, but they

The map above shows an excavated portion of Catal Hüyük. The dotted open areas represent courtyards; the buildings marked by S's, shrines. The tinted area is detailed at right.

An Urban Sprawl of Hillside Houses

To a large extent, the look of Catal Hüyük in 6100 B.C. was predetermined by the shape of the rise on which the city stood—a mound that had gradually grown up as new structures were erected over the remains of old ones. To build securely on such uneven ground, the townspeople constructed their houses cheek by jowl, so that the mud-brick outer walls helped support one another.

The results are reconstructed in the ground plan (above) of a portion of the city excavated by James Mellaart and in the archeologist's conception of how the buildings looked (right). Because the houses were crowded together, terraced roofs, connected by ladders, often served as the town's streets, and entry into the living quarters below was through doorways cut into small second stories.

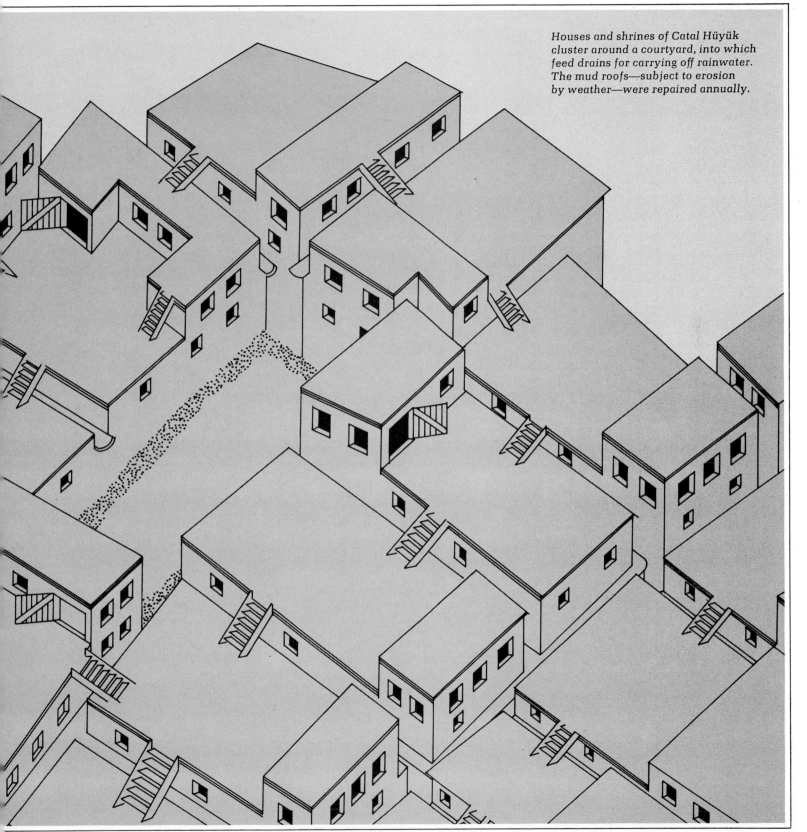

Houses and shrines of Catal Hüyük cluster around a courtyard, into which feed drains for carrying off rainwater. The mud roofs—subject to erosion by weather—were repaired annually.

continued right up to the top." This huge mound, covering 32 acres, was Catal Hüyük, and Mellaart eagerly returned to dig into it as soon as he was finished with the Hacilar project, in 1961.

Far the quickest and easiest way to get a rough idea of the age of a mound, and a sample of its artifacts, is to trench it straight through in a narrow line from top to bottom, digging until virgin soil is reached. So astounding was the size of this site, however, that Mellaart decided to excavate it the hard way, horizontally, uncovering it portion by portion and layer by layer.

It was fortunate that he did, for one of the first of Catal's amazements to emerge was a treasure that vertical trenching might have ruined. A series of wall paintings was still intact after 8,500 years, and a vertical dig might have cut through it. There were enormous red or black bulls surrounded by the red stick-figures of men. There were playful leopards, spotted with rosettes and standing head to head, as well as stags, dancing men in white loincloths and leopard skins, naked acrobats, a man striking a drum, and birds, flowers and hunters.

The murals had apparently been painted directly on the walls with a very fine brush, freehand, by painters who did not need to sketch an outline first. The walls were prepared with a cream- or dead-white clay plaster and then the colors went on strong and vivid: red, brown and yellow ochers derived from iron oxides, bright blue and green from copper, mauve or purple from manganese, gray from galena and black derived from household soot, and all probably mixed with animal fat.

One astonishing painting leaped out at the archeologists: a scene that stretched across the north and east walls of one structure showed several rows of scrawled squares, like a child's drawing of houses (pages 46-47). They were crammed together, rising in tiers. But the astonishing part of the painting was its background, which showed an outline of two peaks spewing parallel lines and dozens of dots.

The archeologists were awed and momentarily baffled, until they remembered the volcanoes outside Catal Hüyük. The painting, they decided, must have been an artist's rendition of a town, presumably Catal, with the twin peaks of the 10,000-foot volcano Hasan Dag in eruption. Hasan Dag is the only two-peaked volcano in all central Anatolia, and it is visible from Catal. No man alive has seen it erupt, because it has been dormant for 4,000 years. But it was active in 6200 B.C. when this painting—possibly the first landscape ever done—was made.

Equally baffling were some other wall paintings showing giant vultures circling over the headless bodies of human beings. Before long the archeologists found a clue to their meaning under the sleeping platforms of the Catal Hüyük buildings. For buried there were human skeletons—most still having their skulls, some of them clothed and some wrapped in light rugs, but otherwise arranged just as they were in the paintings—in either of two positions, flexed and lying on their sides, or extended on their backs.

Mellaart came to the conclusion that the separation of the skulls from the bodies in the paintings must have been meant as a symbol of death, and that the vultures must have been involved in the burial rite. The dead would have had to be stripped of their flesh for hygienic reasons if burial was to be indoors. And vultures would be efficacious for the task, because they will pick a skeleton clean without carrying

A typical house in Catal Hüyük, shown here in a cutaway drawing, was an 18-by-20-foot structure built of sun-baked bricks on a timber frame, with two heavy beams supporting a flat roof made of smaller beams and reed bundles covered over by dried mud. The living space had plastered walls and was subdivided into working and sleeping areas. The man of the house occupied the platform at the rear of the room (1), while his wife and their children slept on another platform (2) adjacent to the kitchen area, which is seen in the foreground. The kitchen was equipped with a low, open hearth (3) and at least one oven with a flat top (4). From the kitchen a ladder led to an opening in the roof, which served as the only entrance to the house and also as a vent for smoke.

the limbs away for consumption elsewhere, as dogs and hyenas do. To this day in Turkey, native vultures —forbidding creatures with wingspans of five feet— perform a useful service in disposing of dead animals in such a way.

The bodies of the dead, Mellaart believes, were probably placed outside the city on high wooden platforms that protected them from dogs and other scavenging animals while exposing them to the ministrations of the vultures and cleansing by rain, wind and the sun's rays. When the time came for annual renovation and replastering of the houses, the skeletons could have been moved to their final resting places under the platforms inside. For they seem to have been buried in groups, and the evidence indicates that some of the bodies had been dead before interment longer than others. Curiously, men were always buried under the northeast platform and women with their children under the eastern platform, the one near the kitchen hearth—suggesting to Mellaart the location of their sleeping arrangements.

The buildings excavated in Catal Hüyük offered clues to more than bed accommodations and burial customs. Of the 139 buildings Mellaart studied, he asserts that no fewer than 40 were shrines. Most of these structures were bigger than the houses but in plan not different; they were equipped with sleeping platforms, hearths and ladders to the roof, like the houses. The major difference was in decoration: it was in these buildings that most of the elaborate art work was found, and the character of the art suggests a religious purpose.

Curiously most of the paintings symbolizing life occurred on the west walls, and most of those symbolizing death occurred on the east walls, directly

Treasures from the Grave

Objects buried with the dead in Catal Hüyük show how sophisticated city dwellers ornamented themselves in 6000 B.C. Among the most popular items for women was jewelry, and for men weapons like the exquisitely made knife opposite. Some were distinguished not only by superb craftsmanship but also by imported materials: flint from south of the Taurus Mountains and sea shells from the Mediterranean.

The three rings above are cross sections of hollow bone. The projection on the ring at center is a natural bone excrescence.

This incised collar was made of a boar's tusk cut in two. The holes were used for lacing the sections together and attaching beads.

A necklace of black and white limestone beads, with two deer's teeth at bottom, surrounds a bracelet of snail shells cut to display their internal convolutions.

This finely executed dagger consists of a flint blade fastened to a bone handle carved in the form of a coiled snake. Showing but few signs of wear, the knife was probably reserved for use in religious rites.

Carved out of bone, the hook and eye (above, left) were used to fasten men's clothing. The buckle-like device at right probably served the same purpose more ostentatiously.

above the burial platforms. Mixed in with the paintings were wall reliefs and benches that are unique for the time. Some of the reliefs consisted of stylized bulls' heads, made of clay but with real horns set in. Some benches were decorated with rows of horns. On the walls, incised into the plaster or built up in low relief, were stylized leopards and stylized women's breasts with massive jaws and tusks protruding from the breasts.

Almost all these reliefs and benches had been painted, and some had been plastered, then painted again with color. It is possible that the white plaster was used to deconsecrate the shrines after they had served their purpose—say the observance of a major festival—and that they were ceremonially redecorated with paint for the next ritual.

Just what sort of rites took place in the shrines nobody knows. Some animal bones have been found in pots in the hearths, and some roasted grain turns up on the hearth walls, as if deliberately burned. But animal sacrifice apparently was not practiced inside the shrines, as there is no evidence of a slaughtering block or a catchment for the runoff of blood. In any case it would have been a feat to get a live animal up on a Catal Hüyük roof, through the entrance hole and down the ladder into the shrine.

Despite the presence of such male-oriented symbols as bulls' heads, Mellaart believes that the main deity of prehistoric Catal Hüyük was female, for a goddess appears in many of the bas-reliefs and paintings. And the ruins also contain 41 little figurines, some in clay and some in stone. Of that number, 33 are female and only eight are male. As in the Venus figurines of the Cro-Magnons, the goddess' face is relatively featureless, but her breasts are bulbous and

Beauty aids found in Catal Hüyük prove that city women wore make-up even then. The shell at upper left held rouge; the red ocher (top, right) was mixed with fat to make it stick. Tapered bones at center were used to apply blue or green ointment as highlights. While making up, a woman would study the effect in a polished obsidian hand mirror (bottom).

her belly is fat and often decorated with paint. One evocative bas-relief shows the goddess with long hair flowing out from her head as if she were in extremely rapid motion. Others show her seated with both legs spread out and both arms extended outward and upward in a sort of caricature of an Oriental dancer. (Mellaart interprets the position as that of childbirth.) Many representations of the goddess show her accompanied by leopards, among the most popular of the shrine beasts; leopards support her arms in the moment of childbirth in one scene, in another leopard cubs rest on her shoulders.

The broad outlines of life in Catal were sketched by Mellaart himself, but he had the aid of a large team of specialists. He recalls with glee his first contact with Hans Helbaek of Denmark, the paleobotanist who identifies from charred seeds and traces of pollen the types of grain prehistoric men used for food, and from this information deduces how and when they began to domesticate it. Helbaek had agreed to work on material from Catal, and Mellaart innocently gathered up several boxes of seeds and grains, cleaned them up nicely and sent them off. Helbaek promptly hit the roof. Nice clean seeds are of little use, he explained: he wanted them just as they had been found, mixed up with all the muck and debris of the site itself.

Thus chastened, Mellaart invited Helbaek to spend a season at Catal. Helbaek duly reported that the paleobotanical finds there were the "largest, richest and best preserved of all early cereal deposits so far recovered," and then he went to work sorting out close to three million individual specimens. Among them he identified 14 types of domesticated food plants, the most common of which were two types of wheat still grown in Europe and Asia, einkorn and emmer, as well as barley, bread wheat and the common field pea. The emmer grains, Helbaek noted, were large and nearly uniform, while the einkorn grains were small and irregular, an indication that they had only recently been domesticated: they had not settled down to the standardized form that is a sign of full domestication. The residents of Catal also knew a species of wild vetch, and they cultivated another form of the plant called bitter vetch, which they probably used in soups. They grew shepherd's-purse and a mustard-like herb for their oily seeds. These provided the plant fat that today is often derived from linseed, sesame seed, cotton seed and the like.

Even more remarkable, Helbaek noted, was the discovery in the ruins of almonds, acorns, pistachios and hackberry (the latter produces a cherry-like fruit from which the Romans later made wine). Neither the nuts nor the berries grew on the plain around the city; their presence is a clear indication that the people had contact with persons or products several miles distant in mountainous country.

This diet was supplemented by milk and meat from domesticated sheep, cattle and goats, and by other meat from hunting. The bones of aurochs—the wild ancestors of today's cattle—also lie in the ruins, together with remains of such other prey as deer, boar and wild ass, and occasional bones of fox, wolf, gazelle and leopard. Other indications of diet can be discerned from analysis of the human bones, and for this Mellaart called in J. Lawrence Angel, a physical anthropologist of the Smithsonian Institution.

Angel studied 288 skeletons of men, women and children from Catal Hüyük from the years 6200 to 5800 B.C. and found signs of an uneven diet in the re-

The mother goddess, shown giving birth, is monumental in appearance but less than seven inches high. The clay figure, found in a grain bin, was apparently meant to foster bountiful harvests. Her head has been restored.

Dramatizing fertility, this stone plaque shows on the left side a god and goddess embracing, and on the right the goddess holding the apparent product of their union, a baby.

A male god, his head lost, is portrayed in brown limestone astride a leopard. Other statues show the same god riding a large bull or as the bull itself.

The Divine Family

The rich variety of religious statuettes unearthed in Catal Hüyük's numerous shrines would seem to indicate that the ancient inhabitants worshiped many deities. But did they?

According to archeologist James Mellaart, who excavated a portion of the city, they are all members of a divine family—mother, father and their offspring, as shown here in various guises. The woman, the most important figure in this pantheon, is sometimes depicted as lithe and young (right), sometimes as a fleshy—and obviously pregnant—mother figure (left). In both cases, her role was that of an all-powerful earth mother, who controlled the supply of game and grain —hence the life and death of the community.

This limestone sculpture stresses the mother goddess' mastery over wild animals: she stands fearlessly behind a sleek spotted leopard and wears a pointed leopard-skin neckerchief.

currence of a slight deformation of the leg bones of some persons. From this he concluded that the residents of Catal Hüyük ate less meat than their nomadic predecessors. He estimated that to get as much meat as those earlier hunters averaged—about a half a pound a day—a city the size of Catal Hüyük would have required 3,000 pounds of meat, for which the residents would have had to slaughter three aurochs, 12 boars or 50 domesticated sheep per day.

Although the shift in diet had already affected the townsfolk's bones, it had not ruined their teeth, which had six times fewer cavities than mid-20th Century American teeth; the Catal people had less than one cavity per person.

One significant observation about teeth had nothing to do with diet: an odd cylindrical groove in the upper first incisor of the women. This kind of wear turns up in human teeth today as the result of smoking a clay pipe or biting on bobby pins. In Catal it probably came from the habit of using the teeth to hold tough reeds while making baskets, or perhaps from biting the butt of some kind of drill used to work wooden household implements.

The lengths of bones told Angel that the women averaged five feet one and a half inches tall, the men averaged five feet seven, taller than their ancestors of earlier periods. They also lived longer, although women lived shorter lives than men did, a pattern that was not to change until the 19th Century A.D., when women in Western civilizations began to outlive men. Their longevity was deduced in part by studying the bone formation, an indication of age at death. In Catal Hüyük, men lived an average of 34 years and a few reached the age of 40; women averaged 30, a year and a half better than the women

Fragments of baked-clay statuettes of a boar (top) and a bull are pieces intentionally broken in an ancient hunting rite at Catal Hüyük. Evidently the damage done to such figures, many pieces of which were found in pits near shrines, was thought to make the killing or disabling of game easier. The fingernail imprints on the boar represent the animal's bristles.

who preceded them. From the inordinate number of female skeletons aged between 15 and 30—the child-bearing years—Angel deduced that many women had died in childbirth. But the addition of a year or a year and a half in their life span was invaluable. It permitted them to produce one more child, expanding the population, and it also allowed them a few more months of maternal care and teaching—of incalculable importance in a society reaching the complexity of Catal Hüyük's.

Angel suggests that the "completely settled and rather secure life of the trading settlement" helps explain the longevity of Catal's inhabitants. But city life did not spare them injury. At least one man apparently was gored by an aurochs during the hunt. Many seem to have fallen from rooftops as they built, and from slippery mountain ridges in their pursuit of game and obsidian. They sprained their shoulders struggling with heavy loads, and from the evidence of their skulls it seems that they must have fought among themselves: no single group of persons until the bellicose days of the Roman Empire suffered so many head wounds.

They also suffered from disease. Angel found signs of childhood sickness in transverse lines across the tooth enamel. This symptom develops when some organic stress temporarily inhibits growth at the crown edge of the tooth. It generally signifies a chronic illness during the first six or seven years of life. Angel also found signs of malaria in the unusual thickness of some of the skulls. He believes it possible that some of the low benches or "sleeping platforms" in the shrines may actually have been used as healing platforms upon which malaria sufferers and other ill or wounded could be placed while the intervention of the gods was invoked. Such healing benches were common in Rome in the Fourth Century B.C., a time when malaria was prevalent.

For all the wealth of information yielded in the excavation of Catal Hüyük, many questions remain unanswered, including the most important one: How did it happen that this diminutive city was so rich?

Excavator Mellaart himself leans strongly toward trade as the answer. Catal Hüyük lay in the region of a major prehistoric source of obsidian, the volcanic "natural glass," which could be used for everything from knives to mirrors, razors and jewelry. It was the most widely traded of all commodities during the period. Mellaart points to the existence of obsidian from the Konya mountains in such faraway places as Jericho, and to the presence in Catal Hüyük's ruins of such foreign materials as seashells from the Mediterranean Sea almost 100 miles to the south and fine flint from northern Syria to the east. There were also foreign nuts and fruit seeds.

Helbaek says, "There is no doubt that the magnificence of the town was ultimately derived from trade." Indirect support for the trading theory may come from current studies of the Catal skeletons by a French expert. Among the ruins were the remains of two distinct types: one of European stock and the other of Asian. Mixed racial types are one of the hallmarks of a city, and their presence indicates movements of different peoples over long distances. The minority groups could scarcely have been invaders in Catal, because there are not enough of them to have overwhelmed the others; and there are no signs the city was ever under siege. The residents were settled folk whose forebears had migrated from elsewhere; and something had to lure them there.

If it was trade that drew them, then did the people of Catal Hüyük trade anything besides unfinished obsidian? Evidently they did. No evidence has been found of warehouses or craftsmen's workshops. Yet the paintings, daggers, stone and wooden bowls, metal jewelry, bone pins, flint daggers, and obsidian mirrors and arrowheads are of such quality and quantity as to attest to the presence somewhere in the city of expert craftsmen to make them. But the excavators found only one sickle and one spindle whorl, and despite the finished obsidian blades and mirrors they found no more than a dozen "cores," the crude lumps from which obsidian articles are made.

Maybe the craftsmen's quarter lies buried in the unexcavated parts of the great mound: Mellaart, by pure chance, may have dug into an elite quarter where the aristocrats of the shrines lived apart from those who wove cloth, cut grain and fashioned jewelry. But there may be another answer to the puzzle. The trade may not have been solely in obsidian and handicrafts, but in intangibles—such as religion. The presence of all those shrines suggests that Catal Hüyük may have been some kind of holy city. It is possible that the excavated acre happened to be the shrine center, and that the skeletons found there were those of priests and priestesses who tended the shrines and were therefore privileged to live in quarters adjoining them.

As a shrine city, Catal Hüyük would probably have had festivals at established times of the year. To these the faithful or the importunate could have flocked from the surrounding area. Perhaps they came piously bearing offerings of flint and seashell that they had acquired in trade from other populated centers that lay beyond them; perhaps they brought semiprecious stones and lumps of sulfur, or acorns in baskets and animals on the hoof, to propitiate the bulbous-breasted goddess and the rows of bulls' horns in the shrines.

These are only some of the mysteries that lie unexplained under the 31 unexcavated acres of this surprising little city. The answers cannot be known until the excavation is completed.

Stirring Settings for Rituals of an Earthy Faith

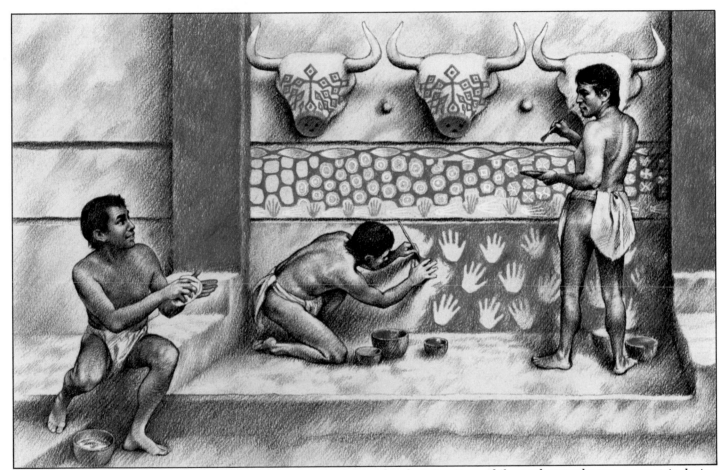

In a shrine adorned with three plaster bulls' heads, an artist paints a handprint pattern while another works on a geometric design.

The original mural survives in this form.

If the excavated portion of Catal Hüyük is any indication, religion was overwhelmingly important in the ancient city. Archeologist James Mellaart identified more than 40 shrines, or about one shrine for every three buildings unearthed by his team.

Though the rites and celebrations held in them remain largely a matter of speculation, the shrines yielded a wealth of physical evidence that was used, with Mellaart's guidance, to recreate, in drawings that begin on this page, four of the town's most elaborate shrines. The scenes are accompanied by photographs of surviving wall paintings or sculptured decorations from the shrines themselves.

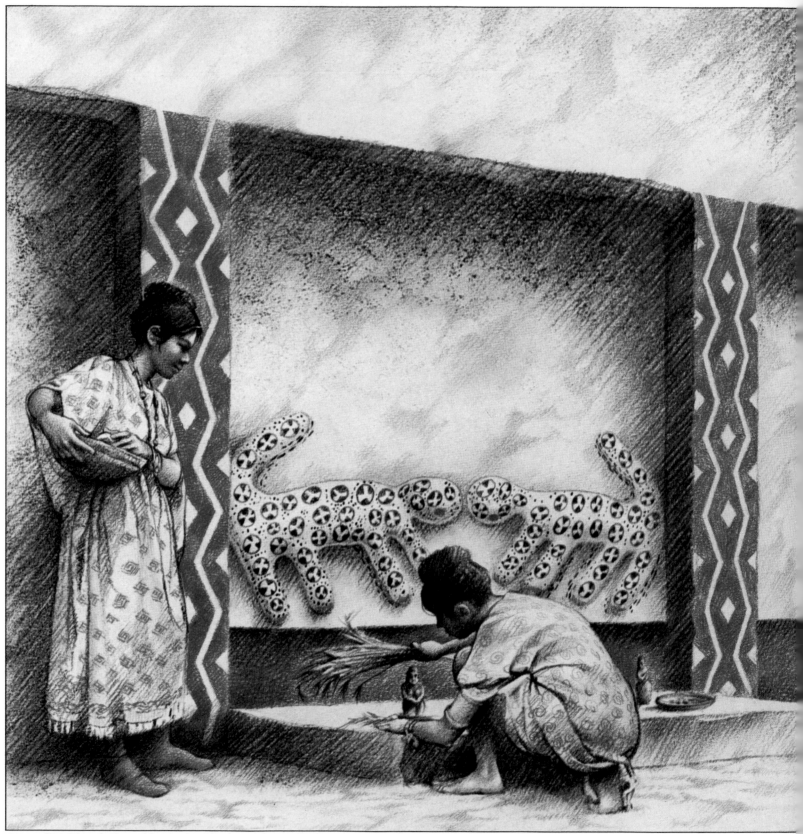

At an altar-like platform blazoned with plaster leopards, two women make a harvest offering, placing wheat spears and a basket of seeds before

At Harvest Time, Thanksgiving in a Leopard Shrine

Stylized leopards protrude from the wall.

In late summer, when crops began ripening on the fertile plain around Catal Hüyük, early samples of the harvest apparently were brought to shrines as thanksgiving offerings to the goddess of fertility. One such offering was made at the Leopard Shrine, so called because it was dominated by two life-sized plaster reliefs of leopards *(left)*, the goddess' animal symbol. In this reconstruction, a sheaf of wheat and some shepherd's-purse seeds, a kind of wild mustard that was used to make cooking oil, have been set beside stone effigies of the goddess. One of the figurines shows the goddess as a corpulent mother figure, the other as a slender young woman.

Burned traces of these gifts were actually uncovered on the low platform which, until a fire destroyed the shrine, had been regularly replastered and repainted. No less than 40 coats of paint were found on the leopards; their spots, seen here as large, fanciful floral designs, appeared in other layers as a scattering of dots and dashes.

statuettes of the goddess of fertility. The men at right are storing larger baskets of threshed grain.

Triumphant hunters admire their trophies and small game while two women prepare a venison feast. The men's ceremonial leopard-skin garments and harlequin body paint are also worn in the murals by figures surrounding two stags and a huge bull.

A Ritual Feast to Celebrate a Successful Hunt

This hunter appears in the mural at left.

A ceremonial meal that would satisfy a modern gourmet was served in celebration when a band of hunters returned home to Catal Hüyük laden with local game, which usually consisted of deer, hare, duck and goose. A typical feast in the Hunting Shrine is depicted here, showing not only what the celebrants ate but also how their cooks prepared the food.

One woman, holding a pot over a flat-topped oven, stirs a stew made with peas and roasted wheat and flavored with herbs, juniper berries and shelled almonds. A second cook takes cubes of raw venison from wooden bowls to her right and broils the meat on skewers over an open hearth. The festive spread also includes a flat loaf of unleavened bread, a basket of apples and pears and a large wooden bowl of hackberry wine. The celebrants probably ate their food from wood plates while sitting cross-legged on the floor, either at the low banquet board or on the mat-covered platforms that border the walls.

The Vulture Shrine: A Place Where Life Met Death

A diving vulture assails a headless man.

The Vulture Shrine, dating to 6000 B.C., tells much about life and death in Catal Hüyük—and implies still more. As archeologist Mellaart interprets its powerful murals, the headless human figures symbolize dead men, and the vultures attacking them are picking the bones clean, a process that permitted burial in shrines or in homes of relatives.

Excavation of the Vulture Shrine laid bare the bones of six individuals who had been buried with grave goods that were markedly richer than those found in the more numerous home burials; this might well be a sign that shrine burial was reserved for wealthy or distinguished folk, possibly members of the priestly class. The grave goods—an elegant assortment appears in the reconstructed funeral at right—ranged from highly prized jewelry to containers of food. These buried objects were apparently intended for future use, and thus they seem to attest to belief in an afterlife among the people of Catal Hüyük.

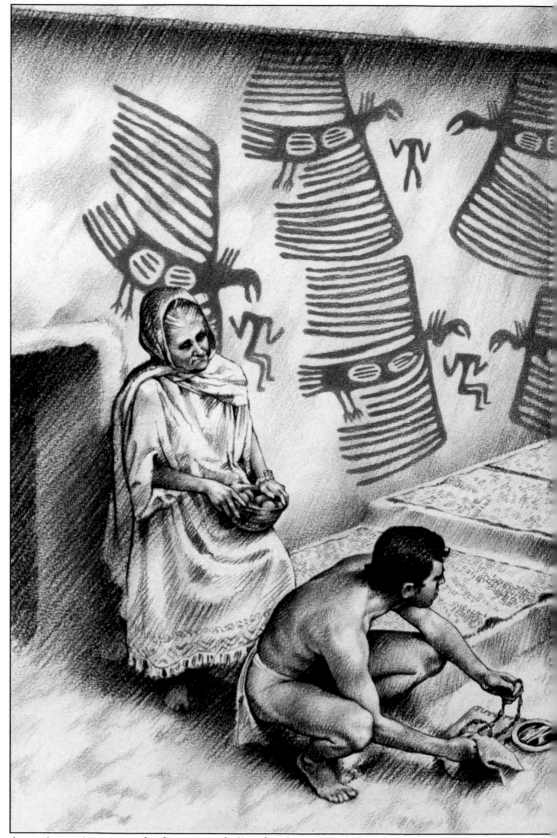
A man (center) anoints a dead woman's skull with ocher—a symbol of the blood of life—as her cloth-

wrapped bones are prepared for burial. Relatives hold gifts: (from left) fruit, a blue-beaded necklace, a mirror, flowers and a carved ivory collar.

Chapter Four: The Homely Arts

In the ancient towns and cities, where all production depended at first on human labor, life could not have been easy—and yet it was here that many everyday conveniences developed. The living standard rose as various crafts—building, stone carving, weaving, pottery making, woodworking—contributed to the general comforts of body and the home. To be sure, the applied arts did not appear all at once, or at the same place; rather, they were thousands of years in coming about, and some originated with nomadic hunter-gatherers. But they flourished in the early cities as they never had before, and the city quickly established itself as the headquarters of homely crafts —the place to go for the newest and best in the things that made life convenient and attractive.

The townsmen's tendency to temper the useful with the beautiful asserted itself very early in their architecture. As long ago as 8000 B.C. the inhabitants of a village called Mureybit on the left bank of the Euphrates River, east of Aleppo, in Syria, paved their houses with limestone slabs, and then some of them carved into the limestone the forms of snakes. This motif may have had superstitious or religious meaning for these peoples; still it represented decoration, a conscious working of the commonplace stuff of a floor. At another town, Cayönü, in southeastern Turkey, archeologists have found a settlement 9,000 years old in which one big room had been floored with polished orange-colored stone chips set in ce-

Unearthed from a tomb in the ruins of ancient Jericho, these 3,500-year-old pieces of bone inlay once decorated the lid of a small wooden box. The elaborateness of the design—four sprightly pigeon-like birds with round eyes, surrounded by incised borders—suggests just how well developed the decorative arts were in this busy oasis trade center.

ment—perhaps the world's first terrazzo pavement.

At Catal Hüyük the residents devised a neat clean plaster with which to freshen their houses every year. In Jericho, builders covered clay floors with a layer of cream or red lime plaster and then burnished it to a high, impervious finish; after more than 9,000 years these Jericho floors can be swabbed quickly and easily with water and will come up as tough and shiny as any housewife could desire. The same builders had also learned the trick of sloping the floor plaster upward to meet the wall, a curving construction that, like the "cove base" of modern kitchens, eliminates the dirt-collecting crack where floor meets wall.

Further enhancing the attractiveness of these early houses were geometric designs painted on the walls, including zigzag lines enclosed in straight ones, and triangles set side by side. The first city folk decorated mainly with red, cream and black—colors that they could obtain easily from mineral sources and soot. Often they outlined the most important elements of the home—the hearth, the ovens or the shrines—with accentuating red.

It was in their utensils and accouterments, however, that the early city dwellers first displayed the imaginative craftsmanship that helped so much to raise the standard of living. They had to have containers for carrying or storing things. They had to have cooking vessels and serving dishes and bowls. And these items they made from every natural source available to them: leather, worked stone and bone, wood, rushes, reeds.

Stone and bone were readily available in most places and were therefore used for everyday objects. In Jericho, before the invention of pottery, the settlers fashioned handsome bowls and plates from native limestone, and at Khirokitia, a 5000 B.C. settlement on Cyprus, they used andesite, a volcanic stone that could be hollowed and shaped with flint and obsidian tools. There is one Khirokitia andesite bowl that was artfully decorated with an incised design on the outside *(pages 74-75)*. It also has a crack down one side, and beside the crack are two carefully bored holes that someone apparently drilled to effect a prehistoric repair: perhaps the mender threaded a bit of tough animal sinew through the holes to keep the crack from widening.

In areas where stone was fairly scarce, as around Catal Hüyük, the inhabitants made containers and dishes of wood. There were oak and juniper on the hills and fir in the mountains. Craftsmen, armed with polished greenstone axes, first rough-cut the wood and then refined it with sharp obsidian blades. Working from solid blocks of wood, they carved whole and clean, with nothing glued on or fitted in later. In all the remains of Catal's wooden artifacts, no joints, pegs or dowels can be found.

These limitations of technique seem only to have stimulated design in Catal Hüyük. Some dishes are circular, some oblong and some boat-shaped. Some are narrow ovals set on feet. There are meat platters 20 inches long, scooped out and flattened out on the bottom to balance. There are wooden containers that look like all the salad bowls in the world—round, high on the sides. And there are egg-shaped goblets —no bigger than today's eggcups—with bases like champagne glasses. Almost all these pieces were cut so that the grain would show to advantage. They could just as well have served their pedestrian purposes if they had been simply whittled out of wood. But Catal Hüyük's craftsmen—and others, working

Baked clay seals with varied patterns were common in Catal Hüyük. The two shown here could have been used for stamping patterns on cloth or decorating human skin. The designs probably were made in wet clay with a stick or bone tool. Most were round, rectangular or oval, but some had a flower shape (top), a design found in certain wall paintings.

elsewhere—became artists in wood, and let the inherent beauty of the material shine through.

In addition to bowls and plates, the woodworkers carved boxes with fitted lids for storing household treasures. In Catal both the wooden boxes and their lids were carved, like the bowls, from single blocks of wood. Many of the lids had small protruding lugs to serve as handles. Similar lugs were carved on the largest of the platter-shaped serving dishes.

At about the same time these craftsmen were learning how to turn wood into useful and beautiful household goods, others were refining the art of basketry and matmaking. Archeologists assume that long before there were towns, hunters had noticed the way shrubs grow together to make near-impenetrable barriers. Indeed, the Australopithecines of three to five million years ago seem to have sheltered at night within confining circles of tangled thorny brush, and Homo erectus apparently knew how to build crude huts of overlapping branches at least 400,000 years ago. Perhaps the hunters had learned to tangle branches on purpose, to form protective coverings or even primitive sledges for carrying home slain game.

Just when basketry was invented—and by whom—nobody knows. It presumably predates fired pottery, and it is thought to precede textiles. The first farmers knew how to entwine river reeds to make mats: from the ruins of 7000 B.C. Beidha, an agricultural village located in Jordan, have come fragments of round reed mats.

The making of such mats is a relatively easy process. First, the craftsman needs a good supply of fairly heavy vegetable stems—weeds, river reeds, rushes, cereal plants. These can be twisted together to make lengths of rope, but if the rope is not to come undone, it must be wound with some lighter, more pliable vegetable fiber called "bast." Once wrapped in bast, the rope can then be tightly coiled in a flat spiral, and the coils themselves bound together with bast passed under and over two of them at a time in a kind of interlocking stitch.

The matmakers' coiling technique is believed also to have been used in the first baskets. The spiral simply became three-dimensional instead of flat—as though wrapped around a bowl. One advantage of the coil was that its circumference could be altered easily to provide baskets of varying girth. While mats generally were produced with just enough bast to hold the coils, baskets usually were completely covered with bast to hold their shape and make them tight enough to avoid loss of contents as small as seeds or cracked grain. Thin layers of clay or pitch were often added to the inside of baskets so that even liquids could be stored or carried in them.

The use of intertwined bast to hold fiber coils together is a kind of weaving. This technique could have led to plain weaving—individual plant fibers of equal size laid at right angles one over the other—but no one knows which came first. Possibly each developed independent of the other. What is certain is that plain-woven baskets and mats—made without coils—appeared very early. The ruins of Catal Hüyük have yielded the remnant of a mat or carpet that had clearly been woven in a classic darning pattern: the reeds were threaded over and under each other, and then pulled tightly together.

It was but a step from this form of matmaking to woven fabrics. For years the oldest known cloth in the world was a fragment of linen, from El Faiyum, in Egypt, a site just south of modern Cairo. El Faiyum, founded sometime before 5000 B.C., lay in an oasis through an opening in the escarpment of the western Egyptian desert. After the discovery of textile there, no one really expected to find fabrics any older. Then, in the early 1960s, small squares of cloth remains turned up in the ruins of Catal Hüyük. They were at least a thousand years older than those of El Faiyum, dating from about 6000 B.C.

Preservation of these swatches of prehistoric fabric is something of a miracle. They come from cloth that had been used to wrap the bones of the dead or to fill a skull cavity for ritual burial. The burial process itself helped preserve the fabric remains: the bones and cloth were interred where they were protected from the deteriorating effects of air—in the clay under the sleeping platforms of houses or shrines. A catastrophic fire in 5880 B.C. destroyed the buildings but preserved the fabrics. Since there was little oxygen in the burial places, the flames could not consume the fragile cloth. Instead, the heat converted most parts of the fibers into carbon without altering their shape—just as wood is converted by heat into charcoal. Carbon does not deteriorate with age, so the carbonized fabrics endured without change through the ensuing eight millennia.

Today these relics of ancient cloth are small, brittle swatches that when scrutinized look like burlap (above, right). Yet the experts who have examined them say that the threads were spun well and evenly, and that the fibers were carefully prepared for spinning. The threads are smooth, with none of the "hairs" that denote hasty preparation or lack of skill, and each lies neatly parallel to the next.

Even more impressive is the fineness of the work. Weavers traditionally define their finished products

A wad of cloth, found stuffed into a skull at Catal Hüyük, is one of the oldest known examples of weaving. Intense heat from a fire around 7,900 years ago turned its fibers to carbon, destroying their identity but preserving their appearance.

by the number of threads per inch of warp and woof. The woven materials from Catal had thread counts as high as 30 per inch in one direction, 38 in the other. The cloth was thus as finely woven as one of today's lightweight wools.

What fibers were used in the world's oldest known woven material is something of a mystery. Fabric experts are confounded by conflicting evidence. The fineness of the weaving, the neatness of the individual threads, the way they lie parallel to one another and the lack of any coarse hairs would indicate that the fibers were vegetable—flax, for instance, used to make linen. Yet in all the millions of seeds found in Catal there is no trace of flax. On the other hand, from Ali Kosh, a village in southwest Iran, comes indirect evidence, in the form of flax seeds, that linen was being used there as early as 6500 B.C.

Microscopic analysis and chemical tests into the nature of the fibers raise more questions than they answer. Individual fibers seem to have scales that look like those of wool, and even after their carbonization the fibers contain traces of chemicals—particularly nitrogen, indicating that they came from an animal source. Still, cloth that has been in contact with the human body can absorb nitrogen from it, and the samples in question had come from cloth that seems to have been worn before being used to wrap bones. One scientist boiled a sample of Catal Hüyük fabric in dilute alkali; the treatment permitted more detailed microscopic examination that revealed cross-striations typical of flax. So this evidence points back to a vegetable source.

If flax was used, it would have required more processing than wool or goat hair. Flax stems must be soaked to decompose the cellular material, and beaten to separate the fibers from the rest of the plant matter. The fibers so obtained must then be combed and spun. Originally, spinning may have involved no more than rolling fibers against the thigh to form a crude thread, but by 6000 B.C., the time when Catal Hüyük's textiles were made, the spindle was doubtless in use (pages 84–85).

Fabric can be woven entirely by hand, as baskets and straw mats are. But looms seem to have been invented at about the same time as woven cloth. Catal's fabrics could have been woven on a vertical warp-weighted loom or a horizontal ground loom (pages 84-85); both were employed in prehistoric times. In its most primitive form the vertical loom probably consisted of a wooden crossbar and two supporting posts set against a wall. The weaver—almost certainly a woman—would wind her warp, the vertical strands of thread, around the bar and let each thread dangle. Then she would take small clusters of these and attach weights at the bottom so they would hang straight down. Weaving consisted of passing a stick loosely wound with the woof, the back-and-forth threads, under and over alternate warp threads.

The ground loom consisted of four pegs driven into the earth, to which two beams were fastened. The warp threads were stretched between the beams. In addition, every other warp thread was tied to a separate stick above one beam. When this "heddle rod" was raised, it separated the warp into two layers, making a space between them, the "shed," through which the weaver passed the woof. To make the next woof row, she lowered the stick and pried up the even threads with a flat piece of wood turned on edge, the "beater," and inserted the woof.

However they were woven, the carbonized swatches of Catal Hüyük fabric are of a simple type called "tabby," the basic over-and-under checkerboard pattern produced by the warp and woof. Some had the woof threaded in very loosely, to make a light, net-like weave. Some were woven so loosely they had to be knotted at the joints. A few had a fringe at the bottom, apparently created by letting the warp ends dangle and then cutting them off well below the last row of woof. There was even one piece with a plain rolled hem sewn in with a coarse, easy running stitch —in and out, up and down. Still another bit of cloth had been mended with a needle and coarse thread in a classic darn, the same kind that chafes the heel when made in a sock today.

These carbonized scraps of fabric lack patterns and give no indication of colors. Yet on walls of ruined Catal buildings are colorful painted designs that apparently imitate patterned textiles. Many resemble the modern Turkish *kilim,* or thin woven rug, and incorporate stripes, swastikas and rectangles filled with triangles in a sort of early Union Jack. Even more evocative of cloth designs, some wall paintings have what appear to be painted-in stitches along the edges —a kind of hem. Because there seems no reason for painters to imitate stitches, some archeologists believe that weaving inspired these decorative wall paintings. It is likely that at the beginning, fabrics were woven plain and then decorated afterward. The clue is the discovery in several ancient cities of little baked clay seals *(page 70).* All have flat bottoms and upper surfaces with incised patterns: flowers, criss-cross lines, spirals and quatrefoils.

When the seals first began turning up, archeologists guessed that they had been used to stamp colored patterns onto human skin. Perhaps they were. But they may have been used on cloth as well. On the wall of one of Catal's shrines is a painted representation of a pregnant goddess who seems to be wearing a voluminous floating garment patterned by the seals. Her body certainly is covered with red, black and orange designs, and the same patterns continue on the wall beside her. The implication is that the image represents a gowned goddess whose garment had been stamped with colored seals.

The weaving of cloth represents one of man's great early accomplishments. Of equal importance was the invention of pottery. Few innovations until the wheel and writing did so much to change the quality of human life as did pottery. It was cheap and easy to produce, and clay could be found almost everywhere. It was handy to use and adaptable to everything from a drinking cup to a five-foot-high storage vessel. The earliest evidence of fired ceramics goes all the way back to Cro-Magnon times, 25,000 years ago, when hunter-gatherers baked figures of clay mixed with powdered bone, for possible ritual use. They never made pots, however; the secret of baking clay to make it permanently hard seems to have been overlooked in the Near East until around 7000 B.C., although unbaked clay pots were apparently used earlier there. The first farmers employed clay to line their hearths, storage pits and probably some of their first baskets. They also shaped crude vessels from clay and sun-dried them. But unbaked pots were too fragile. They cracked or broke if anyone jostled them

or dropped them. Thus pottery had to wait for its moment of glory until men and women had settled down permanently in communities and begun to experiment with ways to make their lives more comfortable, more convenient and more beautiful.

That moment came, in the early cities of the Near East, between about 7000 and 6500 B.C. The bottom, earliest levels of habitation in several of the most ancient sites from Israel to Persia, from Turkey to Mesopotamia, are totally without fired pottery. When finally it arrived, however, it revolutionized life. The process of baking clay provided a quick and easy way to make not only cooking pots and storage vessels, but a host of other things as well, ranging from bricks, lamps and chimney pots to troughs, molds, loom weights and toys. And where stone was scarce, fired clay hoes and sickles served a useful function indeed.

The first potters, like the first weavers, were probably women: women's fingerprints have been found on some of the earliest pottery known in the world. Indeed, they may have been ordinary wives and mothers who made pots as easily as they made bread. In their kitchens they had all the equipment a potter needs except the wheel: a hearth, a small oven, a sharp obsidian knife and tougher, though somewhat duller, cutting tools of flint, a spatula made of bone, a roller of wood.

Clay was easy enough to obtain and the only secret was preparing it well, perhaps by adding some fine sand to temper it. When the clay was of the proper consistency, it could be molded by hand or rolled into coils that could be laid, one on top of another, to form a pot or some other vessel. The pots were then left to dry in the sun until they had reached a leather-hard stage. To make them less porous, they were

Painted Clues to Ancient Fabrics

Although only a few scraps of cloth survive from prehistoric cities, wall paintings in the ruins of Turkey's Catal Hüyük suggest the patterns and colors that weavers may have employed. The designs shown here—the one below is an actual photograph of a painted wall and the other three are copies made on the site—may reproduce patterns found in ancient woven wall hangings. Many similar designs are still used in Turkey today for rugs called *kilims*.

A ruglike mural in a Catal Hüyük shrine incorporates indistinct patterns that are thought to represent stylized flowers and bulls' horns.

Bands of lines, painted freehand, are repeated in a geometric design.

This copy details the left-hand section of the wall painting at left.

Crosslike flowers stand out in dark fields framed by jagged borders.

burnished with a stone; this operation sealed most pores. The firing took place in an open hearth, an oven or, better, a kiln, which provided an improved circulation of heat and ensured a finer product.

With fire-hardened pottery came a tremendous improvement in hygiene. Cooking pots could be cleaned easily. And they could be tossed out if they cracked or chipped. Liquids could be stored in vessels and covered with lids to keep out flies and other insects. And clay storage jars kept valuable supplies of grain safe from rodents whose teeth could gnaw through baskets. So stunning was this great leap forward that many of the gods of the ancient world were likened to potters. The ram-headed Egyptian god Khnum, the creator of all things, was a potter. The Mesopotamian goddess Aruru pinched off a bit of clay to create man. And the Hebrew prophets, in words that readers of the Bible repeat today, said that "we are the clay, and thou our potter."

The first potters, in contrast to the early weavers and woodworkers, were not particularly imaginative folk. Their wares were, on the whole, humble, functional. When the pots were decorated at all, they generally had a few daubs of color swabbed carelessly on them, or checkerboard designs or triangles scratched onto them, reflecting an attempt to imitate simple basketry patterns. Eventually more sophisticated designs emerged, but not until the rise of the civilizations of Mesopotamia, the Nile and the Indus Valley did pottery begin to display major improvements, a reflection, perhaps, of the impetus provided by the invention of the potter's wheel, approximately at the same time as that of the vehicle wheel, around 3500 B.C. in Mesopotamia.

What pottery may have long lacked in refinement,

Two wooden boxes were undoubtedly considered prized possessions, if only because wood was so hard to come by in some early cities of the Near East. The pomegranate-shaped box at top, only an inch high, was found in a Jericho tomb, and was probably carved with bronze tools about 3,500 years ago. The other, about 7,800 years old, came from Çatal Hüyük, and may have been worked with flint or obsidian tools.

furniture soon made up for. As early as 7000 B.C. the residents of Jordan's Beidha had devised rough-hewn sandstone slabs a few inches high that they set into the sandy soil of their village apparently to eat on, thereby keeping the sand out of their food. Similar blocks of stone, or boulders, or even tree trunks must have been the first chairs, although some social historians think the chair began life as a throne and has since come down in the world. According to this theory, only a priest or a king could sit in comfort, while his subjects groveled on the floor in front of him, and the claw feet of an Empire couch are the descendants of gods or godlike beasts that once supported the throne of a monarch.

In the ruins of most of the first towns there is no hint of furniture. There are raised platforms, as in Catal Hüyük, upon which the families sat, slept or perhaps even ate meals together. The first identifiable furniture from the Near East, outside of Egypt, was found in Jericho, and dates from about 1700 B.C. The remains of wooden benches, stools, tables and even a bed turned up inside airtight tombs where they had been preserved through the centuries by the lack of oxygen and by the presence of bacteria-killing gases.

Wood is of course an extremely fragile material (far more so than pottery) and will not last unless conserved in airless conditions. Even then, it may begin to disintegrate the moment that it is exposed. The discovery of the richest furniture trove of all, in a tightly sealed Jericho tomb, set off one of those scenes of high drama and near-hilarity familiar to archeologists everywhere.

It began one afternoon during Kathleen Kenyon's excavation in 1953. It was 4:30 p.m., just minutes before quitting time. The diggers had reached the mouth of a tomb. Common sense said to wait until tomorrow to investigate further, but curiosity prevailed. They rolled aside the stone blocking the tomb and one glance showed that they had hit one of the most exciting finds in the ancient city: a tomb chock-full of wooden furniture.

The panic was on. Before the archeologists' dazzled eyes a thin film of moisture began to accumulate on that ancient, precious wood, moisture drawn from the first fresh air it had encountered for thousands of years. Almost imperceptibly, tiny cracks began to open on the desiccated surface. The furniture had to be saved at all costs.

An urgent SOS to dig headquarters brought a tiny portable generator to provide light, a balky primus stove to melt paraffin wax, and a little saucepan, stolen from the expedition's cook, to hold the wax. Each exposed bit of furniture had to be dusted and then covered, as quickly as possible, with a coating of wax before it absorbed so much moisture that it would be destroyed. The very dimensions of the tomb caused other problems for the discoverers. The entrance was only 24 inches high and 20 inches wide and the interior was crowded with objects that could be crushed underfoot. One by one, five archeologists took off their shoes, scrunched into the smallest shape possible and slipped inside. Even when they were in they had to stay bent almost double, because the tomb was just over four feet high.

The generator chugged, the primus stove roared, eager hands rushed more and more wax and finally, after 1 a.m., the wooden furniture was coated and could be examined. It included a large wooden table that originally had been loaded with food, dishes and goblets to accompany the deceased to the next life.

The table was more than five feet long, the top constructed of a single plank of wood and the legs set into sockets underneath.

Other tombs had yielded graceful little square stools with carved legs and even one massive stool, obviously meant to seat two persons, with legs that had molded feet swelling out into a curve, rather like an animal's hoof. The seats of all had been made originally of cording, and the joints neatly fitted and held together by wooden pegs.

Stool cording had never been found applied to a bed, however, until what became known as "the all night tomb" was opened. The bed in the tomb was occupied. "The owner," Kenyon reported, "lay rather untidily upon it, his legs projecting at the foot, and his right arm resting on the table in a rather macabre manner. It looked like another rather slipshod piece of work by the undertakers, who had dumped the body down somewhat casually." When the bed was examined, it displayed the same expert workmanship as the stools and table. It had been built with two long sidepieces and four crossbars, fitted perfectly, and the marks of its cord stringing still showed.

All of the wood in the tomb furniture had shrunk during the millennia, but it had not shrunk uniformly. Wood experts' measurements indicate that it had shrunk 25 per cent across the grain, and only about 16 per cent with the grain. Thus many tables that now seem too narrow for their length must once have had more practical proportions, and wooden bowls that turned up as ovals in the ruins must once have been gracefully round.

After all the study and analysis of the furniture, one question remained: Why did most of the tables in Jericho have only three legs, two at one end and a third in the center of the opposite end?

A noted amateur archeologist, King Gustav VI of Sweden, explained to Kenyon: Three legs stand much better on uneven ground than four do. That is why, the King added politely, milking stools always have three legs and also why the tripod is such a useful device even in our era.

Living Well in the City

A group of women make coiled baskets with reeds collected from a nearby riverbank.

Working with limited tools, the first city dwellers nevertheless managed to make from simple, readily available materials—reeds, clay, plant and animal fibers, wood—a wide range of useful products. And as the archeological evidence shows, their work was often of high quality, even when the items themselves were intended to fulfill the simplest purposes. Impressions left by mats and baskets on drying clay pots or the earthen floors of houses, for example, reveal not only neat, tight weaving but a variety of basketry techniques.

But despite the growing technical sophistication of the craftsmen, styles and taste remained conservative for a long while. Even as fired pottery began to supersede baskets in numerous households, the decoration on many clay vessels slavishly imitated the geometric designs and patterns of baskets. Pottery also mimicked the appearance of leather and stone, two other basic materials much favored by early craftsmen in the cities.

With time came innovation; many objects were lifted above the level of the mundane to become art. Pottery was enriched by design, wood was inlaid with bone and ivory. For the growing numbers of the rich, life could be led in comfortable and pleasant surroundings that eventually included even fine wooden furniture, so prized apparently that some people had themselves buried with it.

The Making of Practical Pottery

Making pottery was a fairly simple process, and many a woman in the ancient Near East must have shaped it right in her own courtyard and fixed it on her hearth or even in the oven in which she parched grain or baked bread. All that was needed was a temperature between 840° and 1,300° F., hot enough to drive out water and harden the clay. This heat was often achieved by starting a fire with brushwood and then throwing grass or dung on top to maintain it, a method still employed in some primitive areas of the world. If the temperature could be raised to well above 1,000° F., the clay became denser and less porous, producing a pot of high quality.

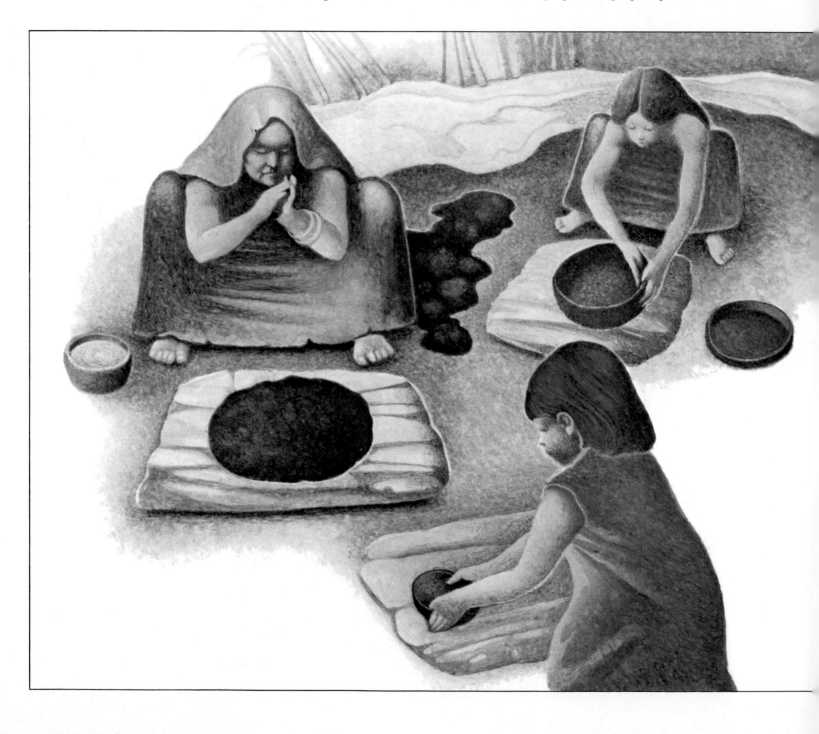

Squatting by the stream bank from
which they have dug their clay, a group
of potters pursue their tasks. The
young girl in the foreground is learning
how to work clay while the other
two shape pots for the woman at right
to bake in a fire fed with reeds.

The Weaving of Fine Materials

Weaving flourished in the first cities, where cloth was produced in homes on a cottage-industry basis.

Although no looms have survived from prehistoric times, a painting on an Egyptian dish of 4400 B.C. and a seal impression of 3200 B.C. discovered in the Mesopotamian city of Susa show the type below. Known as a horizontal, or ground, loom, this early device lacked a true frame, and was set up on the earthen floor of a house or courtyard. As the weaver inserted the crosswise threads, or woof, she inched across the finished portion on her knees, pulling back each new row of woof with a stick. Similar looms are still used in the Near East today.

In a city courtyard a young woman weaves cloth while an assistant makes thread by twisting the raw fiber and paying it out on a revolving spindle. A baby-sitter keeps two children—whose blue bead necklaces protect against evil—from getting in the way.

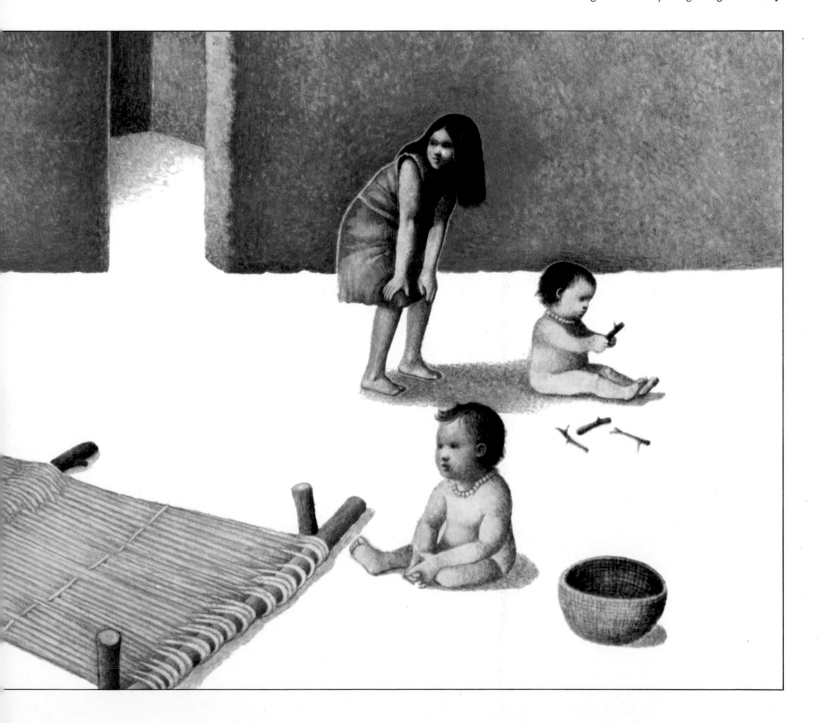

Furniture for the Rich

Judging by the fine quality of the few wooden objects—mostly bowls and boxes—that survive from prehistoric times, woodworking seems to have been a craft to which a great deal of attention was paid by craftsmen.

The pieces of furniture depicted here, along with other examples of crafts developed in the cities, were found sealed away in Jericho tombs dating from around 1700 B.C. The table measured approximately five feet in length and had only three legs, presumably to minimize wobbling on uneven ground. The stools showed remains of cording, as did the narrow bed, which was long enough to accommodate a sleeper five feet tall.

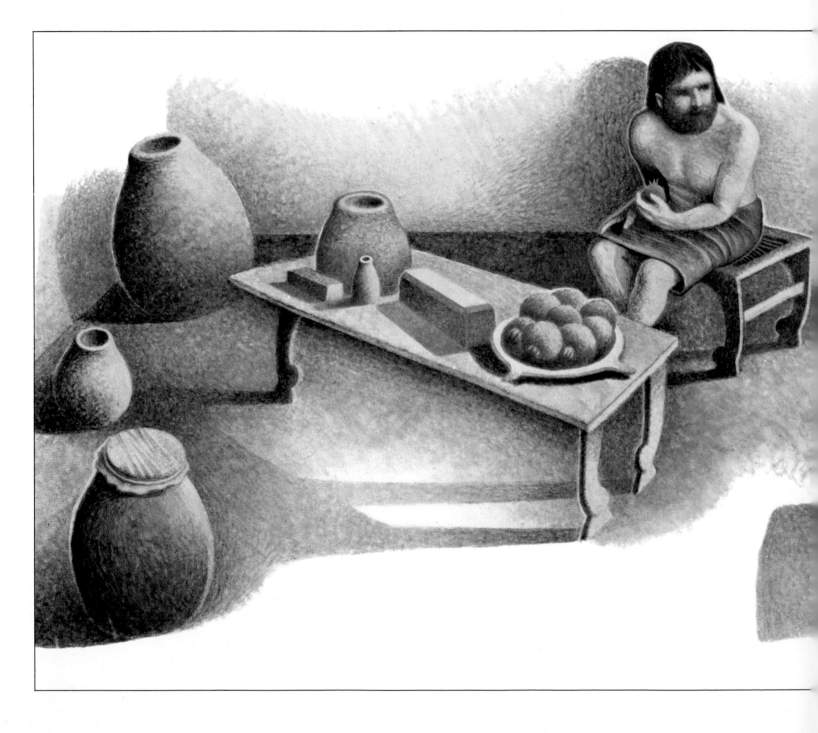

In a scene reconstructed from the evidence of Jericho tombs, a father chats with his son as both munch pomegranates. All the products of city craftsmen—pots, baskets, wooden boxes and furniture—adorn their home.

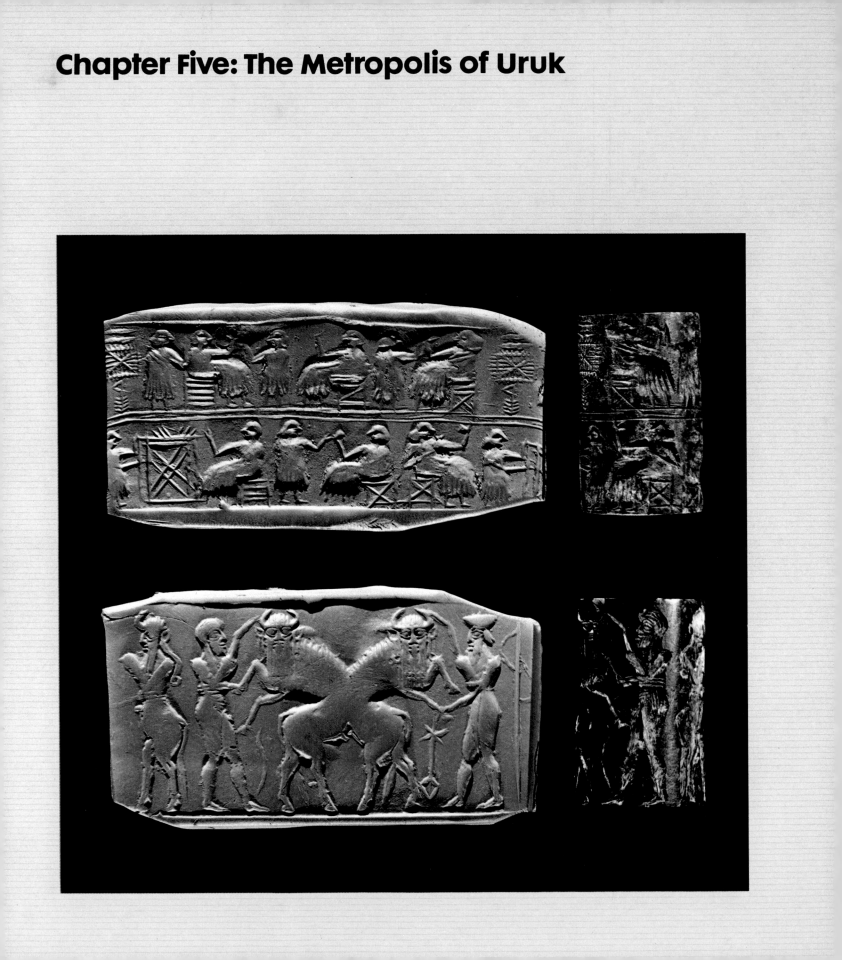

A few thousand years after the first attempts at city life in Jericho and Catal Hüyük—between 3500 and 1800 B.C.—about a dozen far bigger and more complex cities arose on the Tigris and Euphrates rivers in Mesopotamia, today's Iraq. Separately they were city-states; together they formed the Sumerian civilization—a civilization so inventive and so powerful that it gave its name to almost 2,000 years of history and left a legacy that reaches down to the present.

Sumer's cities had all the characteristics the earlier cities had had—division of labor, monumental building, organized religion, satellite agricultural villages providing food—and much more. Sumerian citizens took part in the invention of writing and of the wheel. They helped to develop the oldest known mathematics and obeyed the world's first written law code. Their lofty temples gave men spiritual aspirations, but they did not neglect earthly concerns: crumbling clay tablets from the ruins of temple archives record the payment of grain, beer, meat and cloth to workmen who performed services to maintain the life of the temple, and to indigent widows and children who could not work.

One of the biggest and richest of the Sumerian cities was Uruk (called Erech in the Bible, and Warka in modern Arabic). It was the first city-state in Sumer, and it long remained dominant among a host of obstreperous neighboring cities that vied with each

Before the development of writing, Sumerian city dwellers indicated endorsement or ownership by marks pressed into clay with personal seals—carved stone cylinders like the two that are shown at near left, alongside the imprints they made when rolled over wet clay. Many of the signature designs used religious or mythological themes—the impression at top apparently depicts a funeral banquet, while the other has two "heroes" contending with rearing human-headed bulls.

other off and on for pre-eminence in the region.

When Uruk was at its height, at about 2800 B.C., it was a major city by any standard, ancient or modern. It had a population of 40,000 to 50,000 inhabitants who lived in mud-brick houses. Many were dependent on the palace or the temple, and a few were slaves. But there were also large numbers of wealthy persons and a substantial, prosperous middle class. The houses of the rich were two stories high and had wooden balconies along the upper floors. Even one-story houses of the middle class consisted of several rooms facing central courtyards. These dwellings housed a wide variety of craftsmen —sculptors, scribes, carpenters, metalsmiths, bricklayers, leatherworkers, weavers, potters.

The city at this time in its history can perhaps most easily be seen through the eyes of such a craftsman —say, a sculptor, a man whose name would not have been recorded in the city records, but whose daily routine can be at least partially reconstructed from the mass of records, artifacts and buildings recovered from the ruins of Uruk and its sister cities.

The sculptor's house was whitewashed inside and out (the whitewashing kept it cool in the scorching heat of the Near East), and he renovated it frequently. Like earlier citizens of Jericho and Catal Hüyük, he built his house on the foundations of earlier houses, dating to perhaps hundreds of years before; and his own dwelling would in time be the foundation of yet another house. He rose with the dawn and very shortly went off to his daily work. He left his bedroom through the only opening to the light, a door so low he had to stoop slightly to use it.

The sculptor picked his way through the narrow, unpaved lane that ran in front of his house, then followed similar lanes until he reached one of the broad avenues leading to the main temple. From almost anywhere in town he could see the temple, the dominant monument of the city.

There were several temples, actually. Some were raised upon stone foundations—the first-known temples to have been so constructed. Outside many of them were tall columns of brick faced with a mosaic that glittered red and white and black in the morning sun. Each tiny spot of color was a terra-cotta cone shaped like a nail, its head dipped into paint and then set in the wet plaster covering the bricks. They made patterns of zigzags, triangles and diamond shapes.

Perhaps, as the sculptor passed the temples on the way to his mud-brick workshop, he offered up a prayer for success in his daily work. For he had chosen a difficult profession, one in which mistakes could not be tolerated, because the stone with which he worked was so precious. In all that alluvial plain of Sumer, indeed in all of southern Mesopotamia, there was not a bit of stone, not even a pebble. The raw materials for sculpting—alabaster, marble and a soft stone called steatite—had to be brought at great cost from the slopes of the mountains to the north and east, or from sometimes-hostile lands beyond. A misplaced chisel mark or a badly aimed hammer blow could break a stone and disgrace the sculptor—perhaps even send him to the fields as a water carrier.

The sculptor's failures courted double disaster, since his work was destined for use in the temple and any mistake might be looked upon as offensive to the gods. He made some of the carvings with which the temples were filled—bas-reliefs, figures-in-the-round depicting kings, gods and animals, and ceremonial vases. And in his work he tried to emulate

Two 5,500-year-old terra-cotta statues made by pre-Sumerian settlers in the cities of Ur and Eridu stand slim and straight, with elongated heads and exaggerated shoulders. Their primitive form contrasts acutely with the representational art of the Sumerian civilization only a few centuries later.

the masterpieces of other sculptors. One of the most spectacular examples, an alabaster vase (page 116), was displayed in a temple to the goddess Inanna. The vase, carved with decorative bands running around its face, measured more than three feet tall. The sculptor had often examined it. He began with the top bands showing a procession of nude worshipers, headed by a gowned and tasseled leader, all bearing gifts to the temple deity. He would let his eye wander down to the lowest band showing animals and ripening barley. The whole made an intricate meshwork symbolizing the mystical union of plant, animal, human and spiritual life.

The sculptor was paid by the temple, not in money —still unknown—but in food and fabric for clothing. He had to go at regular intervals and stand in the queue waiting to pick up his ration. But the chore was pleasant. The courtyard of the temple, where the paymasters' offices were located, was a cool refuge from the heat of street and workshop, and there were other workmen in line with whom he could discuss the affairs of the city, the state of the crops or plans for a religious festival.

As it was paid out, each ration was marked carefully on a clay tablet by a seated scribe who used a wedge-shaped stylus to scratch the symbols into still-damp clay. It is likely that the sculptor himself could not read the tablets, but then he did not need to. The literature of his life—the epics of the Sumerian gods and their exploits, the grand stories of the triumphs of kings—were tales passed orally from generation to generation, and the sculptor knew them by heart, having learned them from his father, who in turn had learned them from his father. Sometimes he recited them to his children himself; on temple festival days he took the children to hear the tales from professional storytellers, learned men with sonorous voices.

On a temple festival day the sculptor—or any man of Uruk—must have considered himself highly privileged, a citizen of a mighty civilized metropolis. There were broad avenues, towering temples and grand two-story houses. The streets were filled with prosperous people on their way to worship. Most of the men had flowing, curly beards; most of the women wore their hair braided and coiled around the head. The men were often bare-chested, and almost all wore kiltlike garments drawn tightly at the waist; the women wore form-covering gowns fastened at the shoulders, with their right arms exposed. Many garments were woven of flax and wool; others were of fleece, a convenient and practical covering. Textiles, incidentally, were among Sumer's major exports throughout its life. The streets were redolent with fruits and fresh vegetables from Uruk's adjoining fields: dates, beans, apples, onions, garlic, turnips. Sometimes there were dried fish, pork and duck. And the temple interiors glittered with goods from all the known world: ivory from India, steatite and carnelian from Iran, shells from the Persian Gulf, and lapis lazuli from Afghanistan. It was a wide world in which the sculptor lived, the world of a city man.

The sculptor belonged to a new and expanding class of people who in earlier generations had been village farmers. In the coming generations they were to leave the farms in larger numbers to migrate to the cities and enter the crafts and professions. Some still owned their land, either independently or together with several members of their families. But since 3000 B.C. much of the land had been purchased in large segments—by a wealthy class of aristocrats, by the priesthood for the temple holdings, and by those increasingly important figures in the social structure, the kings, who were amassing royal estates.

In 2800 B.C. the temples still owned a good deal of land. But a large part was held by groups of citizens who bought and sold land as syndicates and corporations. The nature of the syndicates is not altogether clear, although the members may have belonged to extended families whose forebears had once occupied the land in question and had since moved into the cities to take up crafts, like the sculptor. Since hundreds of people might belong to a landholding syndicate, getting all the parties to agree to the terms of a sale must have been a task to challenge the wisdom of a Hammurabi. One fragmented archive of about 2300 B.C. notes that some 600 persons, presumably all sellers, were feasted for two solid days by the other party to celebrate the completion of a transaction. Land values varied widely, depending upon the distance of arable land from the city, the fertility of the soil and the availability of precious water. The values of flocks, of measures of grain and of some metals like silver and gold were well established, and so was the yield of the land; any one or a combination of these could be totted up to a price exchangeable for a plot of land.

The change in land ownership was reflected in the landscape. In earlier periods, settlement in Sumer had been confined primarily to narrow patches along the rivers and to fertile tracts along the margins of swamps. This was enough, however, to freckle the landscape with little mud-brick villages. In the vicinity of Uruk alone in 3000 B.C. there had been at least 146 outlying villages. Each had a temple, irrigated agriculture and a family-clan social pattern.

Beyond the villages lived nomads who drove their herds of sheep and goats from one patch of green to the next and who must have brushed against, or clashed with, the farmers from time to time. If a bad year dried up water holes and scorched the pasture, some nomads were driven to attack the villages; others gave up and sold themselves as slaves.

For protection against these incursions, and for the comparative security of a larger, better-organized place to live in, the villagers drifted toward the growing cities. Between 3000 B.C. and 2700 B.C. the 146 villages around Uruk had dwindled to 76. In the 300 years following 2700 B.C. their numbers shrank from 76 to 24. At the same time the number of cities—in this instance meaning settled places of more than 100 acres—grew from two to four to eight.

As people left the land to settle in the cities, the structure of Sumerian society changed in important details. Its foundation, the family, however, did not alter. From records of land transactions, it appears that the basic family was monogamous and patriarchal; property was handed down from father to son. Women, however, were respected and could attain positions of wealth and power. They had the right to own property, possibly inherited from their husbands. And some records show that women were engaged, on their own, in international trade.

With the drift to the cities, however, came a loosening of the family ties and clan responsibilities that had been so important in the villages. The ties to craft and city were rising alongside those of clan. As a craftsman, the sculptor belonged to a craft group, a sort of guild. Each craft was part of an organized unit identified either by its occupation or by the name of some animal—such as the "snake" group or the

As Sumerian city society became more sophisticated, precious materials and elaborate workmanship were lavished on utilitarian objects such as this pair of rein rings—a device placed on the shoulders of cart-hauling oxen or asses to keep their reins from tangling. These rings, made of silver and topped with the figure of an onager, or wild ass, were found in the tomb of a queen who ruled Ur in approximately 2500 B.C.

"donkey" group—not unlike organized troops of Boy Scouts in the 20th Century.

Members of craft groups had civic responsibilities that went beyond their jobs as sculptors, carpenters and the like. If there was a crisis at an irrigation dam, for instance, they could be called up as a unit and dispatched to make emergency repairs. They could also be asked to help with the harvest. If an enemy threatened Uruk, the craftsmen were conscripted and each guild was put under the command of its foreman. Several platoons constituted a military company and were headed by an officer. For these services, just as for his professional work with stone, the sculptor was paid in food and clothing.

The emergence of a large professional middle class was only one of the social changes that marked the growth of Sumer's cities. At the top of the social structure during the early part of Sumer's life had been the priests and the elders of the city, presumably the heads of leading families. But the Third Millennium brought a transformation of Sumerian society, and the decisions originally made by priests and elders became the responsibility of kings.

Next after the kings, priests and elders in Uruk's hierarchy were the rich—the big landowners and merchants who owned the fleets of ships that carried on extensive sea trade with places as far distant as Bahrein in the Persian Gulf, the Indus Valley cities of Moenjo-Daro and Harappa (Chapter 6), and Egypt. Below these wealthy folk were the bureaucrats and tradesmen. Still another level of society was made up of sailors and farmers, fishermen and water carriers, some employed by the temples, some by the secular aristocracy; and at the bottom were slaves.

Slaves, like kings, were a late development in Sumerian cities; they became increasingly important after 3000 B.C., when there were several cities on the Mesopotamian plain and there was intense strife among them. Most slaves must have been prisoners captured in battle, for in Sumerian, as in many another language, the word for slave derives from the term for foreigner. Other slaves no doubt were impoverished nomads or marginal farmers who sold themselves and their families in bondage to the aristocrats, or to the temple, in return for a roof, a square meal and the security of the city walls.

There may never have been great numbers of slaves in Uruk itself, but their work was important to city life. They were found most often in activities that were specifically urban: in weaving workshops, in bakeries, in the temple complexes, the kings' palaces and the households of the privileged classes.

To judge from the records that mention slaves, most were women. Male captives may often have been killed, perhaps because they were considered hard to handle or because they were feared as a dangerous foreign element within the city walls. It is also possible that the records are misleading; male slaves may have been organized into labor gangs for the military; if so they may have been listed under categories other than "slave."

Clearly the sculptor lived in a far more evolved city than had his predecessors in Jericho and Catal Hüyük. Within the temple complex, there was a stricter division of labor than had existed thousands of years before. The organization of effort that had produced Jericho's wall and Catal's crafts had in Uruk grown into an intricate system with manifold social, economic and political implications.

One thing that sets Uruk off from earlier cities is that its lineage can be traced. Sumer's cities grew from earlier agricultural villages—a fact that led archeologists to believe for a long time that all cities were the linear descendants of agricultural villages. In many places—Jericho, Catal Hüyük and others —this linear evolution seems not to have taken place. In Mesopotamia it did.

The Mesopotamian villages were settled by waves of peoples that came to the plain at different times over many millennia. First, possibly from the southwest, and about 5300 B.C., came the Ubaidians, who founded a village that later became the city of Eridu in the southern part of Mesopotamia. The same people later founded another city, known today as Tell al-'Ubaid (hence their name), in the first half of the Fifth Millennium. Then about 4000 B.C. came Semitic nomads, evidently from the Arabian Peninsula to the southwest, and at about the same time another wave seems to have come in from southern Iran. By about 3500 B.C. all these people had fused into the cultural unit that was to be Sumer.

As they drifted down across the plain of Mesopotamia, they found swamps and marshes by the rivers and their tributaries. When rain fell in fall and winter and mountain snows melted in spring, the waters caused the rivers to overflow their banks and turned the flat land into a flood basin. But in the process of flood and retreat, the rivers had built up natural levees on their banks, created by the silt deposited there. To the lee of the banks were acres of coarse-textured silt, the most agriculturally productive soil on earth. In the shallow ponds of these flood plains were fish and waterfowl. Food was plentiful, and the people prospered.

Unearthed in the city of Ur, this head from a figurine is thought to depict the goddess Ningal, wife of Nanna who was revered as the moon-god and guardian of Ur. The head is of marble, and the gentle eyes consist of shell and lapis lazuli.

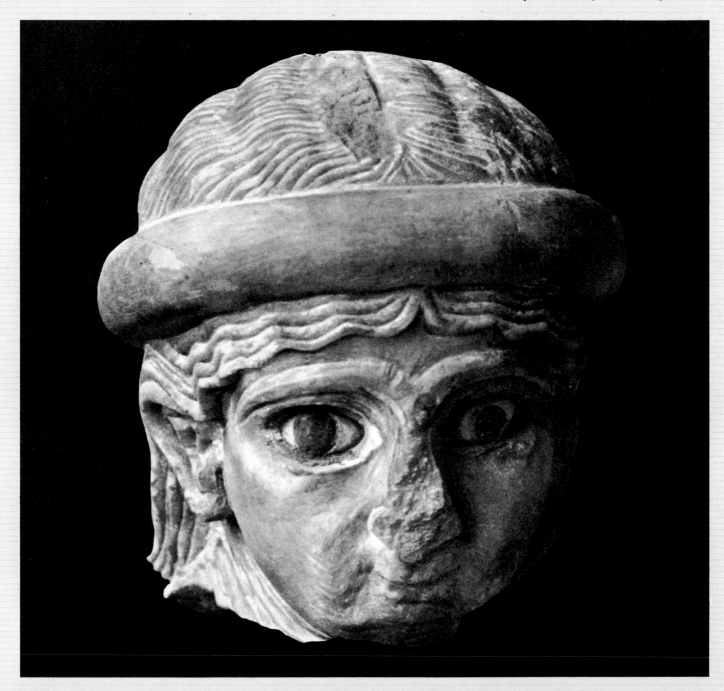

This two-foot clay model of a round
building was found in Mari, on
the Euphrates. Since most Sumerian
houses were rectangular, archeologists
speculate that this eight-room design
may represent a shrine or a fort.

The Ubaidians either brought with them, or very soon developed, a faith in a special deity whose clearly defined duty it was to look after them. But they did not restrict themselves to one god, and in the Third Millennium their successors, the Sumerians, counted between 3,000 and 4,000 deities in their pantheon. Four were major gods, each concerned with one of the then-presumed elements: heaven, air, water and earth. Sumerian gods were conceived as human figures with human concerns—wives and children and bureaucratic problems. An, god of heaven, for example, had a consort named Inanna, and it was to her that Uruk's main temple was dedicated. As chief goddess of Uruk, Inanna was charged with a variety of responsibilities for its welfare, from love to fortune in war. She was also a fertility goddess and patroness of the date palm. The date palm had been added to man's domesticated plants by 3000 B.C., and to Sumer it was a most important one. The fruit was a staple and a choice sweetmeat. In Uruk the date plantations stood within the city walls, the fruit ripening under the very eyes of the goddess.

Religion came to play such an important role in Sumerian life that the houses of worship, the temples, became major elements of the cities. At first, however, they were modest. In the lower levels of Eridu archeologists have found the remains of a temple built about 5000 B.C. It is a one-room mud-brick structure measuring 12 by 15 feet, with an offering table in the center and a niche set into one wall to hold a statue of the god the Ubaidians worshiped. Later inhabitants enlarged the temple again and again. When a temple collapsed from age or weather it was rebuilt, grander and larger than before, and the underlying ruins were shored up with thousands of new bricks to make a new foundation. As the temple grew larger, it acquired more rooms and buttressed walls, but the layout of the nave, altar and niche remained.

With one building rising upon the ruins of another, the foundations of the temples eventually began to resemble giant steps. Perhaps this struck a symbolic note in the minds of the Sumerians. In any case, these massive steps became a characteristic feature of the Sumerian temple, which as the centuries passed evolved into the towering stepped structure known as a ziggurat.

Up, up, up the great steps climbed toward the heavens, crowned always on top by the temple of one or more gods. Bases that began as 50- or 60-foot squares stretched out to 100 or 200 feet and rose 70 feet in the air, about as high as a seven-story building. Some modern engineers estimate it would have taken 1,500 men, working for five years, to construct just the bottom platform of Uruk's ziggurat.

Temples at first were community property, built and maintained as offerings to the impenetrable forces of nature upon which life depended. The pious brought offerings of food and pottery to the gods, and small plots of land were set aside as temple land, thus further to provide for the gods.

Eventually, as surplus food accumulated in the fertile land, the temple took on the function of both repository and redistribution center. It served as a major employer of workmen, as a sanctuary to the refugee and as a source of relief to the needy. Soon after 3000 B.C. a temple at the city of Lagash had a daily ration list for beer and bread for 1,200 men and women, of whom 300 were slaves. It ran a cloth workshop employing 205 women and their children as

The world's oldest known medical text, listing 15 remedies, is inscribed in this 2250 B.C. clay tablet from Sumer. The physician-author—or his scribe—was a master of cuneiform script, as an enlarged detail (below, right) shows. At bottom, two of his prescriptions (for unspecified ailments) are given in free translation.

Pour strong beer over some resin; heat over a fire. Combine this liquid with river bitumen oil and let the sick man drink it.

Sift and knead together: turtle shell, sprouting naga plant, salt and mustard. Wash the patient's sore with good quality beer and water. Scrub the sore spot with all the kneaded mixture; after scrubbing, rub the spot with vegetable oil and cover it with pulverized fir.

carders, spinners and weavers. It had bakers, millers, brewers and cooks. It also employed fishermen, herdsmen, sailors, guards, scribes, blacksmiths and many other workers.

Inevitably the temples came to exert great economic power. At this time they were possibly the cities' biggest entrepreneurs. They not only paid the artists who decorated them, they also mounted their own land and sea expeditions to bring back the soft steatite the sculptors worked, the lapis lazuli and gold used to make jewelry, the limestone for the temple foundations and the timber for the balconies around the second stories of the houses. The cohesiveness of the temple organization, its administrative power and its patronage of the emerging special skills and needs of the city gave it a far-reaching influence.

To keep track of the temples' wide-ranging affairs, the priests and their paymasters and administrators needed records more reliable than memory. To fill this need, the Sumerians took one of the giant steps in all the history of man—they learned to write.

The first writing, about 3500 B.C., was pictographic —that is, simple shapes drawn to represent forms familiar to the eye: a human figure, a hut, an ox, a head of barley. In the act of inventing this representational written language, the Sumerians showed a peculiar genius for using art as shorthand. With a couple of quick strokes they captured the essential form of an object and rendered it instantly recognizable. The first signs were scratched into the wet clay of hand-sized tablets with a sharpened reed. Later the figures became more stylized and were combined with others to express more complicated ideas—in one context the symbol that originated as "foot" meant "to stand," and in another it meant "to go." The tools

became more refined: the sharp reed evolved into a wooden implement with a wedge shape; with it a scribe could make marks in clay that started as straight lines and switched midway to blunt, triangle-shaped ones. And this change in the stylus signaled a great advance in the writing itself. No longer purely pictographic, it became what is today called cuneiform—literally meaning wedge-shaped. Because its characters represented further abstractions, cuneiform was able to express more complex ideas than pictographic writing.

What these first writers wrote were straightforward notations of transactions: "rations," "weaving women," "five." Writing arose from early urban civilization's need for a well-running bureaucracy. In the process it bequeathed to the world the first decipherable record of the way man conducted his affairs.

Mastering the newly invented art of notation and record-keeping was tedious but remunerative. There were organized schools for scribes, and applicants needed impeccable recommendations from someone of importance; it seems likely that as the profession became entrenched it was passed from father to son. Schooling was arduous, requiring years with only a few days a month free—holy days, when students probably had religious duties to perform. The young men had to memorize a series of symbols; as early as 3500 B.C. the written vocabulary of Uruk contained 2,000 different signs. Once a scribe finished school, however, he was assured a position among the upper classes and lifetime employment.

Scribes worked at both temple and palace keeping records. As such they were secretaries and archivists. By 2600 B.C. some were beginning to record and compose epics and hymns—and a few wrote down their

Surrogate Supplicants

The city dwellers of Sumer were a pious people. Eager to please and placate their capricious gods, they first built shrines, then temples, then elaborate temple complexes in which to worship. But the many chores of city life limited their time for praying, so they solved the problem by substituting small statues for their own presence in the temples.

The statues shown below and at right, ranging in height from seven to 18 inches, are typical of the many that have been found. Made of stone, a rare commodity that had to be imported from mountains to the north and east, they preserve an incomparable record of Sumerian clothing and style.

A 4,500-year-old statue of a worshiping Sumerian woman (above), with shoulder-length hair and a simple tunic, was found at Lagash, in southern Iraq.

Bald but full-bearded, the statue at right was excavated from the ruins of a temple to the goddess Ishtar at Mari on the banks of the middle Euphrates.

A queen from Mari, dressed in a voluminous robe, with her hair topped by a domelike headdress, sits reciting her eternal prayers in this stone relic.

A petaled skirt and pious posture characterize this statue from Mari. The sculptor was probably imitating a skirt pattern fashioned from wool.

own experiences, including several reports of sufferings at the hands of teachers who berated their students for ignorance and sloth and beat them on the knuckles if they made sloppy errors. With these accounts the nature of writing made a fateful change. No longer was it a bookkeeper's memory aid; it had become written literature. One student inscribed on a tablet a sad tale of having been caned at least nine times in a day for offenses that ranged from talking without permission to loitering in the street. Another tablet tells the story of a teacher bribed—by a lavish feast, a new tunic and some spending money—into giving good marks to a backward student.

And some scribes became mathematicians; some form of arithmetical record had to be invented, for the rise of mathematics was a corollary to the rise of writing. The Sumerian system of calculation was based upon the number 60—a figure that might seem at first glance an odd base number, but is actually a very practical one because it is divisible by so many other numbers. It survives in many modern measurements today; it is used for dividing the hour into minutes and the minutes into seconds; a multiple of it divides the circle into degrees, and a factor of it divides the year into months and the foot into inches.

At about the same time that the Sumerians invented writing, they also invented that far-reaching technological device, the wheel. It first appeared in about 3500 B.C. Its earliest use was apparently in the making of pottery, to serve in shaping round utensils. But very soon afterward, the wheel was employed for locomotion. It would seem logical that the first wheels should have been single slices of wood cut from a round tree trunk, but nothing like them has been found. In any case, the first known wheels were constructed from three planks of wood—two semicircles fastened by means of wooden struts to a rectangular centerpiece. Together these three pieces made a rough circle. The wooden struts that bound them were later refined into metal strips. Still later, copper bands or studs were attached to the rim to make the wheel tougher and longer lasting.

Among the earliest examples of a wheel is a pictograph of a converted sledge—a platform raised on wheels—on an accounting table found in an Uruk temple. Pictures on pottery and walls indicate that the Sumerians made both two-wheeled and four-wheeled carts. There are also pottery, copper and bronze models of carts in some tombs, and the rotting remains of real vehicles in the royal tombs of Ur.

The axles on the first vehicles seem to have been detachable. This fact implies that much of the terrain was unsuitable for cart traffic and that on long trips the whole vehicle might be disassembled, carried by hand or by oxen to higher, drier or less bumpy land, and then reassembled for the rest of the journey. As a further inconvenience, the four-wheeled carts could not be easily steered, since the axles did not swivel. That idea had to wait another 2,000 years.

Yet crude as the first wheeled vehicles were, they quickly became a boon to farmers, travelers and traders. The benefits were incalculable. An ox or ass hitched to a wheeled cart could pull three times the load it had borne on its back or dragged on a sledge. And it was not long before the cart's possibilities in warfare were recognized.

As villagers had abandoned their communities and moved to cities, large blank spaces developed in the once-dotted landscape, and control over these now

Carved in gypsum, an old couple from Nippur confronts the world of 2500 B.C. with the huge eyes typical of Sumerian sculpture. Its depiction of man and wife with arms linked suggests the importance of marriage in Sumer.

Voices from the Past

From Sumer, the birthplace of writing, have come thousands of clay tablets and inscriptions that do what other archeological remains cannot—they allow the city dwellers themselves to speak. Most are prosaic records, but some are literary works of various kinds—poems, proverbs, essays. Many of these display concerns that still affect humanity today. In fact, the first known use in writing of the word "humanity" crops up in a father's lament to his son, presented in part below, along with other illuminating examples of the Sumerian mind at work.

Law

The following edicts concerning marriage and marital responsibility are from a Sumerian law code of 1850 B.C.

If a man married a wife and she bore him children and those children are living and a slave also bore children for her master but the father granted freedom to the slave and her children, the children of the slave shall not divide the estate with the children of their former master.

If his first wife dies and after her death takes his slave as a wife, the children of his first wife are his heirs.

If a man's wife has not borne him children, but a harlot from the public square has borne him children, he shall provide grain, oil and clothing for that harlot; the children that the harlot has borne him shall be his heirs, and as long as his wife lives the harlot shall not live in the house with his wife.

If a man has turned his face away from his first wife, but she has not gone out of the house, his wife whom he married as his favorite is a second wife; he shall continue to support his first wife.

If a prospective son-in-law has entered the house of his father-in-law and if he made his betrothal but afterward they made him go out of the house and gave his wife to his companion, they shall present to him the betrothal gifts which he brought.

Love Song

The following lines were apparently sung by a priestess to her lover, King Shu-Sin, in a festival held on New Year's Day.

Bridegroom, dear to my heart,
Goodly is your beauty, honeysweet,
Lion, dear to my heart,
Goodly is your beauty, honeysweet.

You have captivated me, let me stand trembling before you,
Bridegroom, I would be taken by you to the bedchamber,
You have captivated me, let me stand tremblingly before you.
Lion, I would be taken by you to the bedchamber.

Bridegroom, let me caress you,
My precious caress is more savory than honey,
In the bedchamber, honey-filled,
Let me enjoy your goodly beauty,
Lion, let me caress you,
My precious caress is more savory than honey.

Bridegroom, you have taken your pleasure of me,
Tell my mother, she will give you delicacies,
My father, he will give you gifts.

Your spirit, I know where to cheer your spirit,
Bridegroom, sleep in our house until dawn,
Your heart, I know where to gladden your heart,
Lion, sleep in our house until dawn.

You, because you love me,
Give me, pray, of your caresses,
My lord god, my lord protector,
My Shu-Sin, who gladdens Enlil's heart,
Give me, pray, of your caresses.

Generation Gap

A father's plea to his son to go to school and learn, assembled from fragments found at Nippur and Ur and slightly condensed here, has parallels with today.

You who wander about in the public square, would you achieve success? Go to school, it will be of benefit to you.

What I am about to relate to you turns the fool into a wise man.

Because my heart had been sated with weariness of you, I kept away from you and heeded not your fears and grumblings. Because of your clamorings, I was angry with you —yes, I was angry with you. Because you do not look to your humanity, my heart was carried off as if by an evil wind. Your grumblings have put an end to me, you have brought me to the point of death.

I, never in all my life did I make you carry reeds to the canebrake. The reed rushes that the young and the little carry, you, never in your life did you carry them. I never sent you to work as a laborer. "Go, work and support me," I never in my life said to you. Others like you support their parents by working.

If you spoke to your kin and appreciated them, you would emulate them. They provide 10 *gur* of barley each—even the young ones provided their fathers with 10 *gur* each. They multiplied barley for their father, maintained him in barley, oil and wool. But you, you're a man when it comes to perverseness, but compared to them you're not a man at all. You certainly don't labor like them—they are the sons of fathers who make their sons labor, but me, I didn't make you work like them.

I, night and day am I tortured because of you. Night and day you waste in pleasures. You have expanded far and wide, have become fat and puffed. But your kin waits expectantly for your misfortune and will rejoice at it because you looked not to your humanity.

Proverbs

Sumerian adages address personal concerns in a surprisingly modern voice.

Marry a wife according
to your choice; have a child as
your heart desires!

For his pleasure—marriage;
on his thinking it over—divorce.

Who has not supported a wife or
child has not borne a leash.

When a poor man dies do not try
to revive him.

When he had bread he had no salt,
When he had salt he had no bread,
When he had meat
he had no condiment,
When he had the condiment
he had no meat.

Wealth is hard to come by,
but poverty is always with us.

Possessions are sparrows in flight
that can find no place to alight.

Don't pick it now;
later it will bear fruit.

Tell a lie; then if you tell
the truth it will be deemed a lie.

Into an open mouth a fly enters.

Who has much silver may be happy;
Who has much grain may be glad;
but he who has nothing can sleep.

Argument

One Sumerian literary exercise was the disputation, in which insults were often hurled back and forth, as in this excerpted argument between two young scribes.

FIRST SCRIBE:

You dolt, numskull, pest, you illiterate, you Sumerian ignoramus, your hand is terrible; it cannot even hold the stylus properly; it is unfit for writing and cannot take dictation. And yet you say you are a scribe like me.

SECOND SCRIBE:

What do you mean I am not a scribe like you? When you write a document it makes no sense. When you write a letter it is illegible. You go to divide up an estate, but when you survey the field, you can't hold the measuring line. You can't hold a nail in your hand; you have no sense. You don't know how to arbitrate between the contesting parties; you aggravate the struggle between brothers. You are one of the most incompetent of tablet writers. What are you fit for, can anyone say?

FIRST SCRIBE:

Why, I am competent all around. When I go to divide an estate, I divide the estate. But you are the laziest of scribes, the most careless of men. When you do multiplication, it is full of mistakes. In computing areas you confuse length with width. You chatterbox, scoundrel, sneerer and bully, you dare say that you are the "heart" of the student body!

SECOND SCRIBE:

What do you mean I am not the heart of the student body? Me, I was raised on Sumerian, I am the son of a scribe. But you are a bungler, a windbag. When you try to shape a tablet, you can't even smooth the clay.

unoccupied areas was hotly contested by rival cities.

The changing conditions of life brought new problems requiring new solutions. When the Sumerian cities had first begun to form, communal decisions had been made by councils of the aristocratic elders. When the need arose for military defense, a city council customarily chose a leader to function as a sort of temporary king for the duration of the emergency. The Sumerian word for king is "lugal," the original meaning of which was simply "big man." The big man selected by the elders would take over, settle the emergency and then return to his own affairs, whatever they were. As cities expanded and the intervals of peace became shorter and shorter, however, the lugal ruled for longer and longer periods of time—and all the while grew more powerful. By 2800 B.C. kings had superseded the elders in political control of the cities.

Yet such was the hold of the temple upon the loyalties of the city dwellers that the lugal always sought the blessing and support of the priests in his conduct of worldly affairs. Often the priests, defending their own prerogatives, helped appoint the king or maintained the right to approve the elders' choice. The king in turn became head priest. He often enlarged and beautified the temple as a means of increasing his stature in the eyes of his subjects and the gods.

Thus were born, in Uruk and other cities of Sumer, two concepts that would influence man's history for thousands of years: the military and political unit of the city-state, and the divine right of kings.

The trappings of royalty, as this institution became entrenched, added another dimension to the already complex social structure of the cities. The kings needed more slaves, craftsmen, bureaucrats, more meat and grain, more cloth and bread—and, as a result of acquiring these, also acquired more control over ordinary citizens. A more complex social structure gave rise in turn to more complex modes of behavior. Sometimes the traditional codes based upon family and clan relationships proved inadequate, or came into conflict. City life produced arguments and grievances as confrontations occurred between different classes with different customs and different ideas about rights and privileges.

As writing came to be increasingly used, more and more men tried to avoid disputes by inscribing on clay tablets their business transactions and deeds of sale. But disputes still arose, for many men also noted on tablets their disagreements with merchants, their indignation with shoddy construction work. Such documents established precedents and could be cited; and it was a natural next step to generalize. Once the Sumerians had done that and committed the generalizations to writing, they had taken the giant step forward—and devised a law code.

This was the code of Ur-Nammu, a Sumerian king who reigned about 2100 B.C. (page 107). His code predates by more than 300 years the code of Hammurabi, a king of Babylon who in about 1750 B.C. set down a series of minutely detailed laws that was long believed to have been the first law code in the world; and it predates the Ten Commandments by almost 1,000 years. A copy of Ur-Nammu's code, made a few hundred years after the original, now lies in a Turkish museum; it was written on a light-brown clay tablet only about four inches by eight inches in size and inscribed front and back. The code established standards of weights and measures for international and domestic trading, and it instituted penalties of

A limestone stele, commissioned about 2100 B.C. by Ur-Nammu, King of Ur and founder of the last Sumerian dynasty, illustrates the Sumerian belief of kingship as a god-given gift. In the top panel, Ur-Nammu is seen saluting a seated goddess; in the second, on the right, he receives symbols of justice and order from the god Nanna, guardian of Ur. In the damaged third panel the King is carrying building instruments. The ladder, in the lowest portion, perhaps alludes to the ziggurat (pages 108-109) that he built at Ur in honor of Nanna.

various kinds for thefts of oxen, sheep and slaves.

The penalties in Ur-Nammu's code were enlightened, generally prescribing fines instead of physical punishment. Some of the provisions, though fragmentary, can be deciphered: If a man cuts off another man's foot, he shall pay 10 silver shekels. If a man severs another man's bones, he shall pay one silver mina. If a man has cut off another man's nose, he shall pay two thirds of a mina.

Laws were not the only legacy of the Sumerian cities to the Western World. In literature can be seen concepts that have come down to modern times almost unchanged from the days when the technique of writing was first put to the service of art and religion. There is for instance the Epic of Gilgamesh, the life of a king of Uruk who lived about 2700 B.C.

Gilgamesh was a terror of a king, a man who chased girls, slaughtered wild beasts, pursued real or imagined enemies all over the country and so oppressed his subjects that they appealed to the gods for help against him. The gods' intervention and a wistful longing for immortality drove Gilgamesh off on an odyssey to seek guidance from the only human being who had survived a legendary flood that had occurred long before his time. The survivor was an elderly man, metamorphosed into a god, referred to variously as Ziusudra and Utnapishtim. Utnapishtim told Gilgamesh of the great flood: he had been ordered by the gods to build an ark, it had rained for days and nights, he had eventually gone aground on the top of a mountain and sent out messenger birds, and finally he and "the seed of all living things" had found a home in the land between the rivers.

One glance at the Gilgamesh epic is enough to astonish a modern reader. Gilgamesh, demigod and folk

The Many-Terraced Ziggurat of Ur

One of the most imposing city monuments of the ancient world is the ziggurat of Ur. Today it stands alone and desolate, a haunt of wolves, in the salty waste of southern Iraq; in 2100 B.C. the ziggurat dominated Ur, testifying to the power of the king who built it, Ur-Nammu (page 107), and to the glory of Nanna, the fabled moon god.

The huge religious center rose in three tiers, an estimated 70 feet above shrines, storehouse, courtyards and the homes of temple staff. Constructed solidly of mud bricks, it was faced with fired bricks set in bitumen—and surmounted, possibly, by a shrine (inset). Three stairways led from the bottom to a gate, and another stairway to the structure on top. Only the crumbling lower tier survives, a massive platform 200 feet long, 150 feet wide and 50 feet high.

A reconstruction shows the ziggurat with ceremonial stairs.

hero to the city people of his era, foreshadowed not only the Biblical story of Noah but also the wanderings of Odysseus and Hercules. The tale was written down first in Sumerian, then in Akkadian, Hittite and, in one variation or another, eventually in almost all the ancient languages of the Near East.

Gilgamesh was immortalized in Sumerian literature; in real life he did his best to ensure his immortality by the same methods his fellow kings used, building palaces that rivaled even the ziggurats in size. One king's palace erected in the city of Mari about 1800 B.C. covered more than eight and a half acres; its central courtyard was paved with precious alabaster. Other, less imposing courts had frescoes portraying deities and the kings' military exploits. Some had as many as 300 rooms for the family, court officials, guards, servants and guests.

When the kings died their tombs were filled with exquisite bowls and other vessels of silver and gold, cult figures made of lapis lazuli and gold daggers done with exquisite artistry. There are decorative pottery figurines of animals, carts and chariots, and ceramic jewelry whose beauty went unequaled for centuries.

In death, however, the Sumerian kings were less than lovable. From the royal tombs of Ur have come not only objects of art but also the remains of ceremonial chariots complete with the oxen, soldiers, guards, musicians and dignitaries of the court; they were drugged and then entombed alive along with their dead rulers. Human sacrifice was a conspicuous feature of the last rites for a monarch; one tomb yielded as many as 74 members of the royal retinue who went to the grave with the king, presumably to be handy for service in the afterlife.

All the same, the cities of Sumer achieved much that would honor any civilization. Their art is spectacular. They invented devices and disciplines that were to carry mankind forward in the succeeding millennia: writing, mathematics and the wheel. They had a specialization of labor that provided employment for thousands. They had a religion that ennobled the spirit and called for altruism. And they had a form of government that organized daily affairs in such a way as to nurture the whole generally admirable culture.

The Flowering of Cities in Regal Sumer

King Lamgi-Mari of the city of Mari appears in a statue honoring the goddess Ishtar.

A key to the glittering success of the urban centers of Sumer can be found in a Sumerian myth of creation. The myth tells how the god Enki, having arranged for the land to be properly watered by the Tigris and Euphrates rivers, laid down detailed strictures regulating life and agriculture. The profound sense of order expressed in this myth helps to explain the Sumerians' genius for organization—from the maintenance of detailed business records and the marshaling of effective armies to the setting up of public works and the bureaucratic administration of city-states and their surrounding countryside.

The framework for Sumer's very numerous achievements was a political system deeply rooted in religion. After 2800 B.C., the local governments in Sumer were firmly controlled by kings—each regarded as the secular representative of his city's guardian deity. As long as a ruler obeyed the divine injunctions to be just, pious and public-spirited, he shared in the popularity of the gods themselves.

But a miscreant king might share instead the fate of Naram-Sin and his city of Agade. In conquering Nippur, this arrogant ruler defiled the temple of Enlil, the leading god of the Sumerian pantheon; and as a result—according to a Sumerian poet—Agade was utterly destroyed in a barbarian invasion instigated by the outraged and vengeful gods.

Ur-Nanshe, King of the city of Lagash, commemorated his works in this plaque. At top he holds on his head a basket of earth (left), symbolizing the start of a temple. At bottom, he celebrates the temple's founding.

Gudea, ruler of Lagash, portrayed in stone

Royal Piety and Public Works

By Sumerian standards, the ruler of a city-state who built public works was generally a good king—i.e., obedient to the gods' commandments. The projects that attracted rulers most and assured them most glory were monumental temples to house the gods. But reality demanded that they also build fortifying walls and irrigation canals.

Ur-Nanshe *(left)*, King of Lagash around 2450 B.C., scattered public works beyond his city's borders; and Gudea *(above)*, who later ruled the same city under the modest title of *ensi*, or governor, built so zealously that he became known as the beloved of Ningirsu, Lagash's city-god.

Sargon *(right)*, founder of the Akkadian dynasty, built on a scale that matched his far-flung conquests, erecting the entire city of Agade. The imperial showplace was a palace large enough for the court's huge retinue of officials and soldiers; Sargon was so proud of its capacity he had inscribed on a statue base the boast: "5,400 men ate bread daily before him."

A bronze head may depict Sargon of Agade

An ax-carrying warrior from Mari

A government official

A prisoner of war

A Talent for Conquest

The Sumerians' talent for organization enabled them to carry out a policy of aggressive warfare. The ruler of a typical city of perhaps 50,000 inhabitants could take advantage of prepared mobilization plans to draft citizens and swiftly expand his standing army for war. The troops, like the society itself, were tightly regimented, with sergeants and officers in charge of companies, and the king in command of all.

Once a victory had been won, it was secured by a systematically ruthless policy. To subjugate the defeated city, the victorious king often crippled its power to resist by selling prisoners into slavery, and then he might install his own occupation government. Yet local patriotism ran so strong that cities often rose quickly from a crushing defeat to fight again.

Advancing behind a wall of leather shields, spearmen of Lagash (top) sweep over soldiers from neighboring Umma in a stele from Lagash. The lower panel shows triumphant infantrymen marching behind the chariot of King Eannatum. The inscriptions describe the battle and its outcome.

A Proliferation of Gods

Sumerian city life was dominated by the gods, themselves organized into a hierarchy that had its own lords and kings. More than 3,000 deities of varying importance were venerated, and each citizen had a personal god, who supposedly interceded for him with more powerful gods.

Originally, the gods were associated with natural phenomena and were depicted in nonhuman forms. Thus Im-dugud, the deity who stood for the force in a storm cloud, was portrayed as a lion-headed eagle *(below, right)*. In time most gods assumed human form; Im-dugud's image, however, became an emblem associated with Ningirsu, patron god of Lagash.

An alabaster vase showing fertility rites

A copper panel depicting Im-dugud, god of storms, with two stags

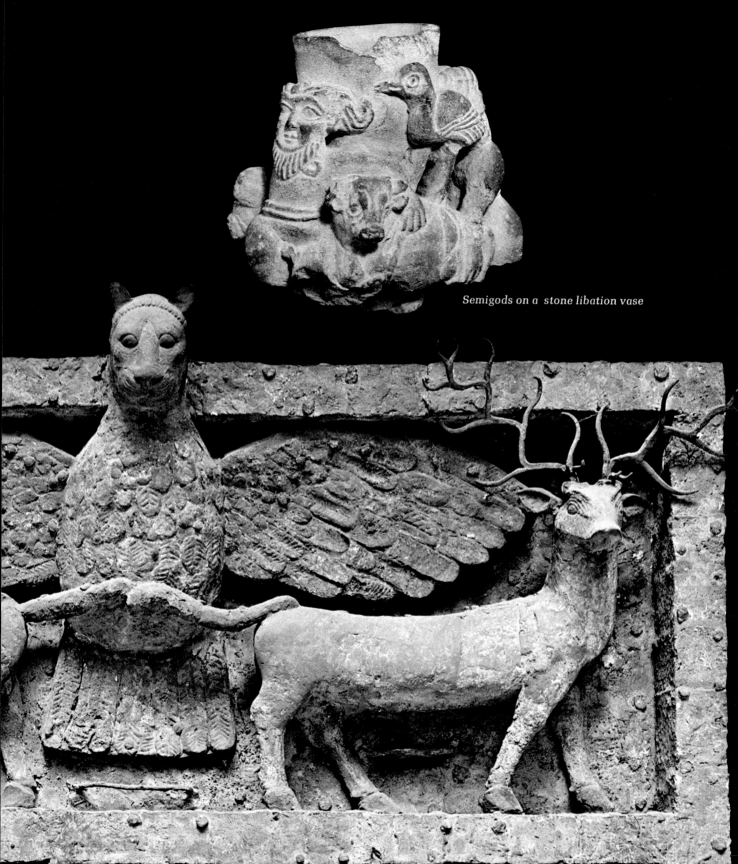

Semigods on a stone libation vase

A professional singer

The Pleasures of Life

Living as they did in a well-ordered society, citizens of every class had leisure time for enjoyment in Sumer's cities. Some people entertained themselves at home, singing to the accompaniment of such common instruments as the lyre, harp, tambourine and reed pipe. Noblemen threw gorgeous banquets and regaled their guests with professional entertainers like the singer Ur-Nanshe, whose pantalooned statue *(left)* suggests that she may also have been a dancer. Even slaves joined in the many public celebrations. The most important festival, New Year's, went on for several boisterous, beer-imbibing days and reached its climax in a re-enactment of a legendary wedding, in which no less a personage than the king himself and a priestess played the divine couple.

But there were also quieter pleasures such as the table game at right, with its elaborately designed wooden playing board, inlaid with lapis lazuli, red limestone, shell and bone—which required more than a little concentration. It appears so complicated, in fact, that modern analysts have not yet figured out exactly how it was played.

A musician playing a lute

A board game with its pieces

Jewelry from the royal tombs of Ur

A queen's inlaid cosmetics box

Luxury Founded on Trade

One important manifestation of Sumer's organizational drive was active trade that brought varied merchandise to the cities and gave artisans the raw materials they needed for their crafts. Because Sumer was poor in natural resources, all precious stones and metals had to be imported from afar in exchange for native grain, wool and cloth. By boat or caravan came gold and silver from Turkey, red carnelian from Iran, blue lapis lazuli from Afghanistan. For the cosmetics box above, lapis and sea shell were inlaid in silver; the shell may have come from fabled Dilmun, believed to be the island of Bahrein in the Persian Gulf.

The Sumerian artisans who created such rich objects operated in small guildlike organizations and ranked among the finest in the ancient world. Smiths beat gold into thin foil and fashioned it into flowers and leaves *(top left)* for jewelry, chasing or stamping in exquisite details. They also made castings with complicated molds, soldered gold to other metals and did filigree work with a richness exemplified by the gold dagger sheath at right.

A courtier's gold knife and sheath

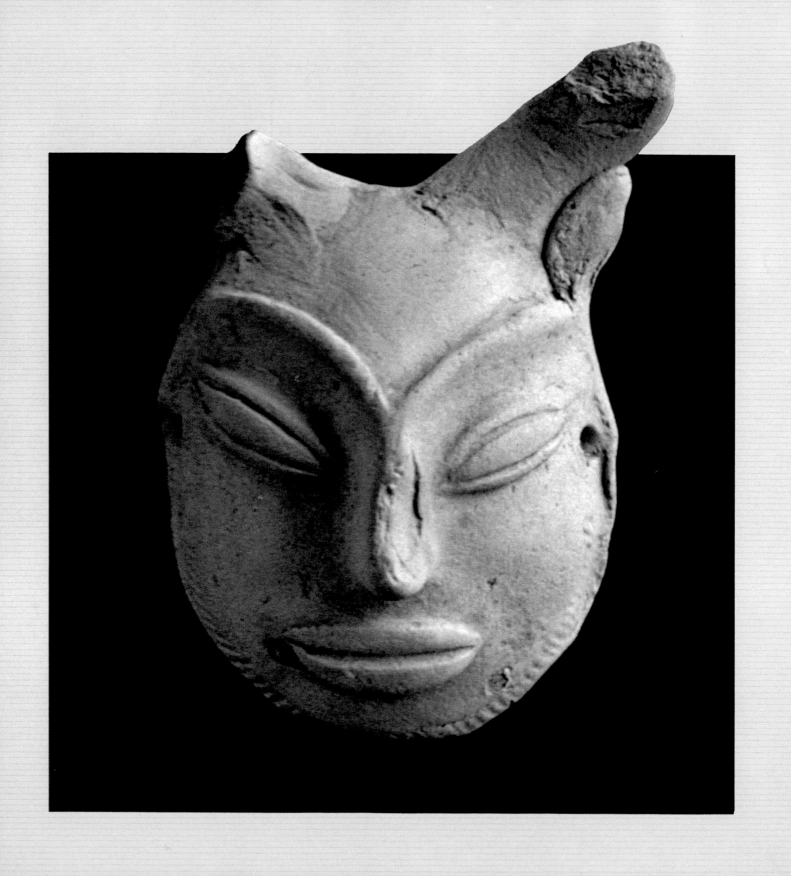

Probably the very first "first city" in which a 20th Century visitor could have found his way around without the aid of a native guide was Moenjo-Daro. It lay on the flat, hot flood plain of the Indus River 300 miles north of today's Karachi in Pakistan. As a busy seaport and trading center that was connected to other cities by overland and water routes, Moenjo-Daro would have been familiar in more ways than one. As long ago as 2500 B.C., it and the half-dozen other cities of the Indus Valley had already put to use the crisscross gridiron system of street layout —an urban convention long thought to have been invented by the Greeks of a later era. Moenjo-Daro was planned with a broad boulevard 30 feet wide, running north and south, and crossed at right angles every 200 yards or so by somewhat smaller east-west streets. Along these impressive avenues were shops and food stands. The blocks between were served by narrow curving lanes five to 10 feet wide.

The grid layout is only one indication of the perception and care that had gone into the planning of the city. Houses presented blank walls to the streets, an architectural scheme that persists today in much of the Near East for protection against the sun, prying eyes and thieves. Most doors were on the lanes behind the main streets, and they opened into entrance rooms with porters' lodges adjacent to them. Interior courtyards provided light and air, and windows were screened with grilles of terra cotta or

This 4,000-year-old terra-cotta mask found in Moenjo-Daro illustrates the mystery that surrounds many artifacts from the first cities. Only two and one half inches high, it combines human and animal features—bull's horns, a beard and slanted eyes. A hole on each side suggests it may have been tied to a wooden figure that has long since disintegrated.

alabaster. Most houses had stairways that sometimes led to the roof—often used today in Pakistan and elsewhere in the East as a cool sleeping space—but in Moenjo-Daro the stairways might also have served to lead to a second story with bedrooms.

But of all the amenities provided by Moenjo-Daro and the other well-laid-out cities of the Indus Valley, none were more sophisticated than those that were devoted to public hygiene. Never before, and never again until Greek and Roman times, was so much attention paid by human beings to sanitation. Running along the sides of the streets were neat, brick-lined open sewers much like those in old Asian cities today, and at intervals there were catch basins dug below sewer level to trap debris that might otherwise have clogged the drainage flow. Archeologists excavating these basins have turned up all manner of artifacts from clay body scrapers, used in bathing (page 147), to terra-cotta toys (page 125) lost by their young owners four millennia ago.

The sewers were connected to each house by an open gutter, also constructed of brick, into which emptied the house drains, which generally consisted of an enclosed system of clay pipes. Two of the houses that have been excavated contained sit-down toilets—imposing structures of brick. They were not simple commodes, but were connected to the drains; whether these outlets led to the sanitary sewer system cannot be determined now, however. The sewers seem to have been built mainly to drain away used bath water. Many houses had bathrooms, their floors built of waterproof brick and fitted with drains leading directly to the sewer pipes.

But the most conspicuous monument to Moenjo-Daro's concern for cleanliness was the Great Bath. A complex brick structure two stories high, it was one of the most massive structures of Moenjo-Daro and a triumph of engineering. The bathing pool was sunk into the paving of a courtyard approached from both north and south by flights of brick steps with wooden stair-treads set into asphalt. The pool, 39 feet long, 23 feet wide and eight feet deep, was made watertight by an inner facing of bricks set on edge in gypsum mortar, which was laid over an inch-thick layer of asphalt troweled onto double brick walls. The floor sloped to an outlet that led in turn to an arched drain tall enough for a man standing upright.

Just north of the pool were eight smaller bathrooms, each measuring about nine and one half by six feet and drained by little runnels in the floor. The bathrooms were carefully constructed along a corridor with the entrance doors staggered for privacy; each room had its own staircase leading to the second story, which may have provided living quarters for people closely associated with the Great Bath.

These elaborate arrangements for personal cleanliness were probably not inspired by any knowledge of hygiene. Ceremonial bathing is an important ritual in many religions, and the Great Bath was probably built for just such a purpose. The public may have used the big pool for ritual cleansing, with the private baths nearby reserved for some privileged class or the priesthood.

That the Great Bath had some ritual purpose is indicated by its location. It stood amid other imposing structures that were apparently involved in religion and government atop a walled citadel: a man-made brick- and dirt-filled platform, 40 feet high, 1,200 to 1,500 feet long and 200 to 300 feet wide, with bastions and towers running along its perimeter. Further

separating the citadel from the residential section below was a 500-foot-wide gap at its base. In this gap there is no sign of habitation. The area may have been a river that has since dried up or changed course, or it may have been a canal. One reason for supposing so is that the east side of the gap, bordering the residential part of the city, is rimmed with nine-foot-thick walls that stand at least 25 feet high and may once have stood higher. Similar walls in Sumerian cities such as Nippur suggest that these in Moenjo-Daro may have served as docks or quais where trading boats tied up.

Among the other buildings on the citadel, the most unusual is next door to the Great Bath. It was more than 150 feet long, 75 feet wide and probably three stories high, but its oddest surviving feature is a series of five-foot-deep, crisscrossing channels in its floor. The archeologists who first excavated a portion of the building thought, from the looks of these, that the channels might have been the remains of hot-air heating ducts or drainage channels of yet another bathing establishment. However, a similar structure on the citadel of Harappa, Moenjo-Daro's sister city 400 miles to the northeast, turned out not to be a bath at all but a huge granary. By analogy, Sir Mortimer Wheeler, a leading authority on the Indus Valley civilization, concluded that the building on Moenjo-Daro's citadel must also have been a granary. Sir Mortimer likened it to a state bank—a secure storage place for grain which, before money was invented, was used as a medium of exchange. Other scholars contend that a building of that size, large though it seems, could not have stored sufficient grain to serve as a bank for Moenjo-Daro's population of more than 40,000. Perhaps it held only religious

So many pottery toys like these were found in Indus Valley cities that some authorities have suggested they were manufactured for export. They were ingenious: the bull has a movable neck and the ram has wheels; the ball is a rattle and the jar with holes (lower right) an insect cage.

That leisure activities found their way into city life in the
Indus Valley is indicated by these artifacts. The stone balls
(upper left) were probably used in play. Next to them are
stone marbles, possibly for a maze game like the one shown
at bottom. The dice (lower left) are made of baked clay
and were unearthed in great numbers at Moenjo-Daro.

offerings, or grain that was marked for shipment.

Whether it was a bank or not, the building was as impressive a feat of engineering as the Great Bath. What at first appeared to be hot-air or water channels are more likely to have been ducts designed to ventilate the storage areas above and keep the stocks of grain dry—for wheat keeps almost indefinitely unless moisture allows fermentation to start. On the north side of the building was another curious arrangement: a long platform with a neatly paved alcove. The platform might have been the loading and unloading dock, and the alcove a bay that ox-drawn carts could enter loaded with grain.

In addition to the granary and the Great Bath, there were several other large buildings on the citadel. One of them, measuring 230 by 78 feet, surrounded a 33-foot-square court, off which were numerous chambers; it has been called the residence of an official or high priest, and is thought by some to have been "a college of priests." Another building seems to have been a kind of reception hall; it is 90 feet square, and is divided into aisles by brick piers. Adjacent to it was still another, somewhat smaller hall.

Leading down from the citadel was a grand staircase, 20 feet wide, constructed of bricks. The residential district spread out to the east. Though most of the buildings in the area were private houses, some plainly served other functions. A structure 250 feet long with a north wall ranging in thickness from three and a half to seven feet could have been a public building. Another, consisting of 16 units arranged in two rows, with a passageway down the middle, may have been workers' barracks. Each unit had two rooms, possibly a bedroom and a living room —but even in these modest quarters, almost every apartment had a corner with waterproof bricks and a drain for bathing.

A third building, much too large to have been used for a family dwelling, is one of the most puzzling in the city. It contained one room that is curious for more than its size; it had five strange conical pits sunk into the floor to cradle large jars. The jars could have held hot and cold food, for they are similar to food dispensaries of a later period that have been found in the ruins of Italy's Pompeii. Sir Mortimer thought that the place was a fabric-dying shop, the jars serving as the dye vats. But another remarkable feature of the building is its floors, which are made of waterproof tiles like those found at the Great Bath. Could this mystery building have been yet another place for human cleansing?

The purpose of many of Moenjo-Daro's sophisticated structures is only one of many questions that still remain unanswered about the city. The discovery in the 20th Century of so complete and so advanced a metropolis came as a complete surprise to scholars, who had never dreamed that a full-fledged civilization had existed on the Indian subcontinent as early as 2500 B.C. It was not until 1920, when archeologists got around to excavating Harappa, 400 miles from Moenjo-Daro, that the existence of a whole network of oddly modern ancient cities was suspected.

Harappa was a pitiful wreck when excavators finally started to uncover it. Railway engineers had been there ahead of them and mined the site in the middle of the 19th Century, digging out its ancient bricks to use in the roadbed of the Lahore-Multan line then under construction, unaware that they were destroying priceless evidence of a past they did not even

The Mother Goddesses

The disproportionate number of statues of women in the ruins of Moenjo-Daro's houses lead archeologists to believe the inhabitants venerated a female deity—perhaps a mother goddess. As befitted a supernatural personage, she was depicted in terms transcending ordinary experience —adorned with lavish jewelry and spectacular headdresses, or endowed with a figure exaggerated beyond reality.

This terra-cotta figurine, crudely fashioned from lumps and loops of clay, is enhanced by decoration with rich jewelry suitable for a goddess.

The prominent breasts, narrow waist and broad hips of a headless goddess wearing a stringed girdle are exaggerated features that also crop up much later in works of Hindu sculptors.

The top-heavy headdress and short, belted skirt of this standing figurine are typical goddess attire. The side pieces on the headdress are both hollow.

This boldly executed terra-cotta bust of a goddess is crowned with an elaborate headdress, only part of which survives. Traces of soot inside the cuplike portion suggest the figurine may have been used as a votive lamp.

know they had. Local villagers, hunting for easy building material for their own houses, almost finished the job of destruction. Even so, enough Harappan remains survived, in monumental structures and delicate jewelry, in graveyards, pottery and tools, to whet archeologists' appetites for more.

Shortly after Harappa was found, the relatively pristine ruins of Moenjo-Daro turned up. In the years since then, British, American and Indian archeologists have worked on more than 150 Indus Valley sites. About half a dozen can be called cities. They show a remarkable uniformity and cover an astonishing geographical spread, from the Arabian Sea to the foothills of the Himalayas and from the eastern border of Iran to the valley of the Ganges near New Delhi in India.

Who were the founders of this far-reaching, long-vanished civilization? Scholars believed that the people of the Indus came down into the valley from foothills of the mountains of Iran to the west, much as some of the Sumerians' forebears came down onto the Mesopotamian plain from the mountainous regions beyond. And like their near-contemporaries in Mesopotamia, the founders of Moenjo-Daro and the rest of the Indus Valley civilization soon achieved specialization of labor, public works, high skill in the applied arts and a written language. The language remains undeciphered despite many attempts, including some using computers, partly because there is so little of it to work on.

In all the Indus Valley, no clay tablets, no temple inscriptions, not even graffiti have been found. The only writing appears as incised inscriptions on a few spear points, pots and other artifacts as well as on a great many small pieces of stone that also bear pic-

tures carved into them (pages 136-137). Most were made with little rings on the back, like the loop on the back of a modern button, as if they were to be threaded on thongs and worn by their owners —which, if literary sources are to be used as a guide, they were. More than 1,200 of these stone objects have been found at Moenjo-Daro alone, and because there are few duplications they are thought to be signature seals. The undeciphered characters appearing with the pictures may have been the names of the owners, and they seem to have been used to make duplicate impressions on clay, which may have been used to label bundles of grain and other goods being shipped in trade. In fact, the existence of so many seals is one reason for believing that Moenjo-Daro and other Indus cities were commercial centers.

Also dug up with the seals was another kind of evidence of trade—weights and measures (page 134). Standards of weight are vital to formal exchange, and the weights that have been found in Moenjo-Daro indicate that its citizens had an elaborate system covering a wide range of goods. Made of limestone, chert, steatite, slate and gneiss, the weights come in a graduated series of sizes. Some are so tiny that they could have been used by jewelers to measure gold or possibly by grocers to measure spices. Others are so big that they must have been hoisted by ropes; these weights must have served to measure large consignments of threshed grain or heavy chunks of ore-bearing rock. Along with the weights there was also found a bronze bar that could have supported a wooden scale beam long since rotted away.

For carrying on their trade, Moenjo-Daro's citizens had several means of transport. Most important must have been wheeled carts and oxen—for among the ar-

Naked except for a necklace and stacks of metal armlets, this four-and-a-half-inch figurine of a saucily posed dancing girl is one of the few bronzes discovered at Moenjo-Daro. The curly hair, thick lips and flat nose are common characteristics among some people who live today in southern India.

tifacts of the period are many toy carts and oxen made of clay. It seems likely that these people also had the camel, though only a single camel bone has been found. They also had boats—which were reproduced in art as well as toys. One signature seal shows a vessel looking much like the gondola-shaped craft that occur in other ancient drawings from Egypt to Sumer to the island of Crete. An Indus boat also appears on a Moenjo-Daro terra-cotta relief and on a potsherd. All these boats seem to have been propelled by sails or stern sweeps. Such craft could have been used for river traffic in the Indus Valley, but they probably traveled a good deal farther; dhows of similar design today sail the same waters that border India and Pakistan. No doubt boats of the Indus Valley sailed up the north coast of the Arabian Sea to the Gulf of Oman, and from there up the Persian Gulf to Mesopotamia, for Indus Valley seals have been uncovered in the ruins of Sumerian cities.

Indus trade went overland as well as by sea. Considerable business was certainly carried on with the hinterlands of Baluchistan to the north. And some authorities believe that an overland route was also used for part of the Indus commerce with the Mesopotamian cities of Sumer, possibly by way of the kingdom of Elam, which lay between the two great centers of civilization.

One of Elam's principal cities, Tepe Yahya in southeastern Iran *(pages 12-13)*, seems to have been a caravan city which grew up because it was situated on the east-west trade route. It certainly traded with the Mesopotamian cities, and it may also have dealt with the Indus, for among its ruins was found a pottery fragment bearing the impression of an Indus Valley seal—indicating that Tepe Yahya had contact

132

The domineering, austere quality of this handsomely dressed and barbered figure carved from steatite suggests that it may represent a deity or a priest-king who ruled over the Indus region.

Found lying in front of the ruins of what is believed to have been a temple, this smiling limestone head from Moenjo-Daro could be a sculptor's representation of a deity. The almond-shaped eyes were once inlaid.

Figures of Authority

Although male figures rarely appear among sculptures dug up at Moenjo-Daro and Harappa, the few that do all seem to represent men of importance. In the three works reproduced here, there is a common theme, however varied the pieces themselves may be: regality or godliness. The sophistication of the torso below—perhaps that of a young deity—has led some scholars to compare it to Classical Greek sculptures of 1,500 years later.

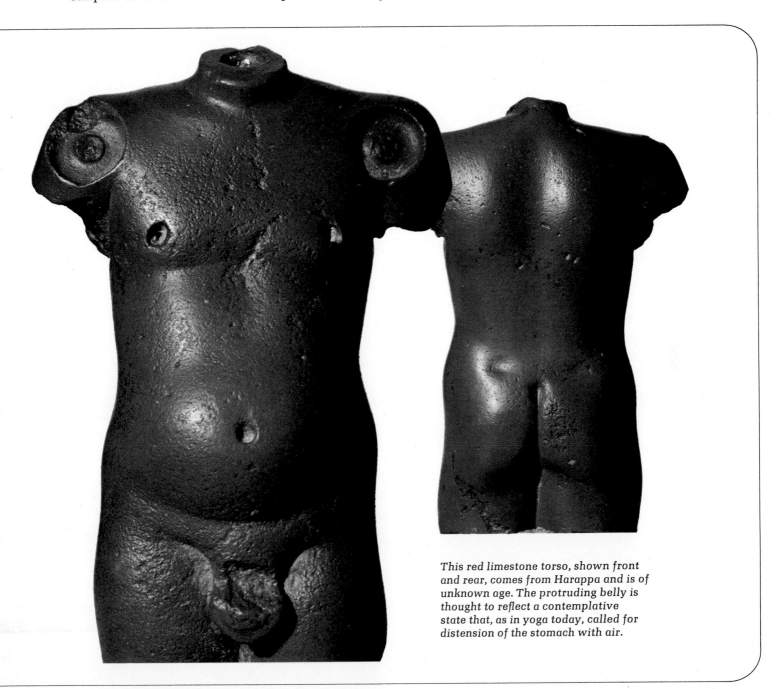

This red limestone torso, shown front and rear, comes from Harappa and is of unknown age. The protruding belly is thought to reflect a contemplative state that, as in yoga today, called for distension of the stomach with air.

A collection of measuring devices from Moenjo-Daro testifies to the importance placed upon precision and accuracy in this city. The weights, generally made of chert, were cut according to strict standards, apparently under control of a central authority, and were used for weighing everything from jewelry to spices. The broken ruler that lies to the right of the reconstructed scale may have been employed in the making of furniture; it is marked off at exact intervals of .264 inch.

of some sort with the civilization lying east of it. A neighboring city, Shahr-I-Sokhta, some 250 miles to the northeast, manufactured a wide range of luxury items of alabaster, lapis lazuli and other semiprecious stones and sent them to cities east and west of it, including those of Mesopotamia, about 750 miles away.

Other excavations undertaken far from the Indus Valley have also shed new light on its civilization. Finds in the Persian Gulf, for example, appear to explain some puzzling references on Sumerian clay tablets to Dilmun, Meluhha and Magan—three cities that early diggers could not locate. The Sumerian inscriptions refer to all three of these places as sea-trading lands of legendary riches lying to the east of Sumer. The new evidence indicates that the Dilmun of the ancient texts was almost surely the island of Bahrein in the Persian Gulf, on the direct sea route between Sumer and the Indus Valley. Magan, the investigators believe, was the coastal area near the Gulf of Oman and Tepe Yahya. And Meluhha, which ancient Sumerian writings clearly describe as a seaport area, may refer to the twin cities of Sutkagen-Dor and Sotka-Koh, now far from ocean access, inland near the Indus Valley.

The idea of there being seaports in a region where today there is no navigable water puzzled archeologists, and yet there was evidence of seaports in the form of representations of ships on Indus Valley seals and terra cotta. But every site that should have been a seaport was not on the sea.

There was, for instance, the ruined city of Lothal, which had an enigmatic structure 730 feet long and 120 feet wide, with what appeared to be a sluice gate at one end. By logic the structure should have been a dock, and among the city ruins lay a Persian Gulf seal of a type usually marking cargo coming from the Persian Gulf and the cities of Mesopotamia. Lothal today stands isolated even from river channels, in mud flats 100 miles from the Arabian Sea.

In addition to Lothal, there were three strange fortified sites, one of which is as far as 350 miles from the Indus Valley, inland from the north shore of the Arabian Sea, lying between Karachi and the Iranian border. Each of these sites had unusually heavy walls, some 30 feet thick, and sturdy rectangular towers. These massive fortifications appear to be strong points meant to defend the surrounding area from invasion—but the walls would not have been able to stop wide-sweeping invaders who came by land. The defense works seem to have been raised against marauders coming from the sea—except that the sites do not lie on today's shore. One of them, Sutkagen-Dor, lies 30 miles from the present coastline; another, Sotka-Koh, is eight miles inland, and a third, Bala Kot, 12 miles inland.

The discovery and analysis of these landlocked ports represents a stunning display of detective work on the part of archeologists and their allies, the natural scientists. For their deductions went far toward explaining a handful of other mysteries connected with the Indus Valley civilization that had baffled archeologists for half a century. The biggest mystery was what caused the demise of Moenjo-Daro.

As in the classic mystery novel, the story begins with the discovery of the body—the city itself—and the presumed cause of death. Most scientists had formed the tentative theory that the city had battled throughout its life against seasonal flooding of the Indus River and its tributaries. As evidence of flood-

136

Testimony of the Seals

Of the many artifacts dug up by archeologists at Moenjo-Daro, few have proved so informative, yet so tantalizing, as the seals. Meticulously carved on small pieces of soft stone (usually with pictograph script at the top), the scenes on the seals provide insights into religious practices, and an occasional glimpse of everyday life as well *(lower right)* —while the ciphers tease by defying all attempts at translation.

The seals were used to make impressions in clay identifying personal property—much like the Sumerian cylinder seals *(page 88)*. They may also have been worn by their owners as amulets with some magical import.

A three-faced deity seated in a yoga-like position (above), possibly a prototype of the Hindu god Siva, is surrounded by wild animals. He wears a horned headdress, and his supple body is adorned with numerous bangles, bracelets and necklaces.

A seal depicting a rhino (above) before a "sacred trough" indicates that offerings may have been made to the beast. So accurately rendered is it, with beady eyes and body warts, that it may well have been a familiar presence in the Indus Valley.

A tree deity (right), hovering between two branches of a pipal—the "Tree of Wisdom," still sacred in India today—is attended by the kneeling figure of a mythical bull-goat and a row of seven pig-tailed women.

The animal most frequently portrayed on the seals is this one-horned beast (left), perhaps the legendary unicorn ascribed to India by Aristotle. It is always shown before a stand thought to be an incense burner, indicating a role in a religious cult.

Carved with close attention to detail, a Brahman bull displays its characteristic hump and neck folds. The same species is held sacred today in India, and may have been similarly venerated in Moenjo-Daro.

A chipped, rectangular seal with an everyday motif (right) shows how river boats were built. The craft has a shallow draft and cross-lashing on bow and stern, which may signify reed construction. In the center is a small cabin and on the right can be seen part of the steering oar.

ing, they cited the fact that every level of the city lay under quantities of water-deposited silt and clay, some of it in layers as thick as six feet. After each catastrophic flood subsided, the theory went, the incorrigible citizens of Moenjo-Daro neatly built again on top of the mud that was left behind—until they could do so no longer.

As one city level was built on another, architecture deteriorated. The houses in the buried lower levels were firmly constructed, spacious and well appointed; those on the upper levels were makeshift, and many were subdivided. Some of the last residents even went so far as to build huts around the proud podium of the great granary, using old bricks instead of new ones.

Thus it appeared that Moenjo-Daro had lost a battle against the river, dissipated its energy, gone into decline and eventually collapsed. The coup de grâce, Sir Mortimer Wheeler suggested, might have been delivered by the Aryan invaders who are known to have swept over the Indus Valley sometime after 1500 B.C. and whose exploits are recorded in the Rig-Veda, the Hindu scriptures. One of the world's great religious epics, the Rig-Veda tells how Aryan conquerors descended upon the "land of the Seven Rivers" in Pakistan and breached the ramparts, shattered the citadels and slew the citizens.

Some evidence for this possibility seemed to exist in the skeletal remains of about 40 unburied and untended corpses that were found at the upper levels of the city—though even to Sir Mortimer these few seemed a pitifully small number of last defenders for such a large place.

Enter the detectives. The first to question the accepted version of Moenjo-Daro's demise was an Indian scientist, M. R. Sahni, who in 1956 pointed out evidence for a dramatic change in the face of the land sometime in the Indus Valley's history, a change he asserted was attributable not to the normal silting, erosion and delta-forming of the rivers but to something out of the ordinary.

The next to tackle the mystery were Robert L. Raikes, a hydrologist noted as a consultant to governments of arid countries, and Robert H. Dyson, an archeologist at the University of Pennsylvania, who analyzed observations compiled by Raikes and other scientists. Raikes and Dyson began by casting their scientists' eyes upon the visual evidence.

The bottom layers of Moenjo-Daro did indeed lie buried under 30 feet of silt, and at first both men had no reason to challenge the view that the silt had taken about 1,000 years—the life of the city—to accumulate. Yet there was no more silt on top of that 30 feet. Why was it that in 1,000 years the city should have acquired such a heavy load, and then in the ensuing 3,500 years received no more?

Raikes turned his attention to the much-admired drainage system of the city, designed—archeologists had formerly supposed—not only to cope with human hygiene but also to handle flooding from heavy rains. It was, as the archeologists had said, a marvelous construction. Raikes estimated that it was capable of carrying off an annual rainfall of about four inches (the average annual rainfall of the area today)—but only if that four inches fell gradually over all the year.

Rain in the Indus Valley falls in sudden sharp storms, however, and these are concentrated in the summer months. There is no evidence that the climate has changed dramatically since 2500 B.C. A

These objects, found in Moenjo-Daro and carved of bone, shell and ivory, are thought to have been inlays that decorated the wooden furniture of wealthy citizens. The wood itself was long since disintegrated, so no one knows how the furniture looked, but its elegance must have been much admired both by Moenjo-Daro residents and by foreigners. Texts uncovered at Sumerian cities suggest that inlaid furniture was imported to Sumer from the Indus Valley some 1,500 miles away.

single rainstorm, if it lasts an hour, can dump a full inch of water on the site. That would be quite an unusual cloudburst, so Raikes began his calculations by assuming a more modest precipitation rate of a third of an inch in a 20-minute storm. He estimated that Moenjo-Daro's closely packed houses and citadel complex presented 80 per cent of the city's surface to the sky in the form of roofs. The runoff from roofs during a 20-minute storm would reach 150 cubic feet per second. And the drains of Moenjo-Daro simply were not constructed to take such a load of water.

This was clue number one. If the drains could not carry off an ordinary summer storm, they certainly could not carry off the waters of a rising river. So they clearly were designed to handle household wastes, not floodwaters.

Clue number two came from analysis of the silt by Raikes and his colleague George F. Dales, who was then Curator of South Asian Archeology at the Museum of the University of Pennsylvania and is now Professor of South Asian and Near Eastern Archeology at the University of California at Berkeley. The silt was too deep, too homogeneous, to have been deposited by a river in flood, even so sluggish a river as the Indus. It looked instead like the result of "ponding"—that is, deposits from an enormous reservoir of muddy, silt-bearing water that stands almost stagnant for years at a time.

Clue number three came when the work of hydrologist Raikes was combined with earlier studies that had been made of cities outside the Indus Valley proper. Dales had excavated the now-inland sites of Sotka-Koh and Sutkagen-Dor, just north of the coast. From the seaward orientation of their defense fortifications, Dales judged them to have been former

seaports, but that raised the obvious question of why they lay inland. Raikes realized that there were many such puzzling sites all over the Indus Valley—apparent seaports now far from water. So he made a hydrologist's study of aerial maps of the Indus Valley and of the archeologists' maps as well.

Two startling facts emerged: One was that the archeologists' maps showed no traces of ancient civilization anywhere along the present-day banks of the life-giving river, from its present mouth to a point 90 miles upriver. The second was that the aerial photographs showed at least 10 prehistoric beaches, identifiable by the concentric crescent configurations of the soil, lying roughly parallel to the present coastline but several miles north, on dry land above and behind the sea.

This clue was decisive. Either the sea had sunk —for which there is no evidence whatever—or else the land had risen. Raikes now believes the latter to be true; he thinks that at least one large section of the Arabian Sea coastline has been forced upward in a tectonic shift—a readjustment of the earth's crust. The upthrust occurred on the seacoast, and the turmoil was felt for miles away.

One of the many dramatic effects of this tectonic shift was that underground gases were churned up by the tremors. They finally erupted, building a land barrier that blocked the flow of the Indus River to the sea and dammed its waters in a large, deep pond that slowly—over a period of many years—backed up toward Moenjo-Daro. As the waters of this huge lake lapped over the foundations of Moenjo-Daro's buildings, their owners built the foundations higher. Structures badly damaged by the encroaching water were leveled and used as platforms on which to place

Decorations carved into a steatite box lid (top) and an ax head (above) from Tepe Yahya, a city of the Elamite kingdom lying between Mesopotamia and the Indus Valley, hint that its citizens carried on active trade with both civilizations. The eagle on the lid resembles an Indus Valley motif, while the one on the ax shows kinship to designs in Mesopotamia.

new buildings, high enough to be dry. Thus Moenjo-Daro became a city in a marshy lake whose water level varied with the seasons, but year after year steadily rose. As the water rose, the city had to rise too. And as it did, its lower levels were drowned in the silt that slowly settled out of the still water.

Raikes's hypothesis has been supported by later findings. Evidently, the entire area bordering the Arabian Sea in both Iran and Pakistan is subject to the extrusive and eruptive activity of "mud volcanoes," the result of tectonic shifts, which force their way, slowly and without volcanic fireworks, through cracks in the underlying rocks of the area. They account not only for sudden uplifts inland, but also for the appearance of new islands in the sea. Such an eruption, recorded in 1819, brought a 15-foot rise in a strip of land 30 miles long and 15 miles wide near Hyderabad. It blocked the branches of the Indus River and caused a 2,000-square-mile flood that lasted for two years. As recently as 1945, several new "mud islands" have risen in the Arabian Sea off Pasni.

So one of the culprits was found: an upward land shift that probably occurred slowly over a period of years. It changed the coastline, shutting off from the sea what had once been beaches and ancient seaports, leaving them stranded.

Farther from the coast other changes attributable to tectonic activity raised land where there had been no land before—the present-day 90-mile stretch of river extending more than half the distance from the sea to the site of Moenjo-Daro. In all this long strip of land there is no sign of ancient towns because when the Indus civilization was at its height, the lower end of the present river valley lay under the water of the Indian Ocean. Today the Indus River, which

Varied Wares of Metalworkers

Metal weapons, tools and ornaments from Moenjo-Daro attest to the skill of the city's craftsmen. Using either copper mined in mountains hundreds of miles to the west of the city or bronze made by mixing copper with tin from the north, they made many of these objects by pouring the molten metal into molds, letting it harden and then refining the castings.

Ornament

Razor

Blade

Ax blade

Spear point

Blade

Blade

Blade

An array of artifacts reflects the versatility of Moenjo-Daro metalworkers. The long blades at bottom right were spearheads; the S-curved hook was for fishing; the large hook beside it for goading elephants. A leaf-shaped blade (bottom left) may have served in ceremonies. The inscription on the curved, tapering blade (bottom, third from left) may be an owner's mark.

Arrowheads

Double-hook tool

Elephant goad

Fish hook

Ring and bracelet

Razor

Blade

Blade

Blade

Spear point

constantly changes its course, runs almost three miles east of the site of Moenjo-Daro, which used to lie right on the banks.

The "mud volcano" phenomenon also helps explain the depths of silt that lie inside Moenjo-Daro, and the city's eventual abandonment. Moenjo-Daro's citizens did not spend their lives, as used to be thought, coping with ordinary seasonal floods; instead they fought a continuing battle for many years against a sea of encroaching mud. As the water level continued to rise, the citizens of Moenjo-Daro built defenses against the accumulating muck, raising walls and drains again and again. As time went by, they took to frugally reusing old bricks instead of making new ones, which accounts for the shabby construction in the later levels of the city. Meanwhile they were exhausting all their other resources as well —physical, economic and emotional.

In the narrative of humanity's achievements and experiences, however, the saga of Moenjo-Daro is dramatic not because of the number of years it lasted. What once appeared to be a gradual degeneration, the decline of a proud city into an urban slum, becomes in the light of recent interpretation the dogged, heroic struggle of a people to defend their city against forces far too powerful for them.

As the river became clogged with mud, their seaport became isolated from the sea, and their very streets filled with slime, the people nevertheless managed to build and rebuild Moenjo-Daro for hundreds of years. When at last they gave up, they may have moved to Harappa or dispersed to other outposts of their cultural domain—south to India, northeastward into the Punjab and the foothills of the Himalayas.

But in the meantime they had learned a great deal about city life, things other men were not to learn for centuries. Evidently they had developed organized means for ensuring the peaceful conduct of everyday affairs—some sort of law system. For along with those handy sewers, Moenjo-Daro had little one-room guardposts built into the corners of intersecting thoroughfares, where "policemen" were presumably installed to help keep order.

Moenjo-Daro must also have been among the first places in the world to provide its citizens with a broadly based, comparatively high standard of living. Most of its people seem to have lived in considerable comfort, in near-identical mud-brick houses, along near-identical streets that were served by near-identical drainage systems. The ruins of residential areas struck one archeologist as "miles of monotony." But that monotony suggests, in its uniformity, an even distribution of material goods among a large segment of the population, and thus the well-being that goes with a large, prosperous middle class.

In Moenjo-Daro people had come a long way from the first embryonic cities of Jericho and Catal Hüyük. They had learned to weigh individual freedom against group security. Some had swapped physical labor for the rewarding torture of mental and creative effort. Most had loosened family-clan ties to drift toward those of profession and class. In the process they had begun to benefit from the towering achievements that characterize urban civilization: literature, mathematics, law and a sense of the greater grouping of mankind. They had, in short, come at last to the delicate balance of freedoms, the poignant day-to-day compromise that has characterized city life from their time to our own.

The Benefits of Urban Planning

Ruins of buildings and streets mark the citadel, Moenjo-Daro's administrative center.

Nearly 4,000 years ago, in Pakistan's Indus River Valley, Moenjo-Daro, one of the world's first truly modern cities, came to an end. The people of Moenjo-Daro had enjoyed 600 years of urban prosperity; but then they succumbed, apparently to mounting natural vicissitudes. The city itself, left to collapse into ruins, lay unremembered and buried in river-borne silt and its own rubble of tumbled bricks until 1922, when an Indian archeologist set out to investigate what he thought to be a Buddhist temple complex. To the surprise of the whole scholarly world, he began to uncover a prehistoric metropolis.

Archeologists have since excavated much—although by no means all—of Moenjo-Daro. What has come to light testifies to the city's high level of urban sophistication. Laid out on a grid system—like New York, Chicago and Los Angeles—Moenjo-Daro's straight, parallel streets were lined with buildings of weather-resistant fired bricks. At its peak, the city's population reached some 40,000; the more prosperous of Moenjo-Daro's residents lived in expansive mansions. What is thought to have been a central granary may have served the community either as a state bank for the government to store a reserve of grain or as a repository for tributes from citizens. And residents enjoyed such niceties as a large public bath and a municipally maintained sanitation system.

A Palace for Bathing

The great bath, set among Moenjo-Daro's stately public buildings, was the city's most impressive edifice. It probably served for both commoners and priests to perform ritual washings; an upper story may even have housed the priesthood. The bath owed its splendor to construction rather than decoration. Engineered to withstand the weight of tons of water, it was made of bricks laid in perfect alignment; an English archeologist remarked that he could not even slip a visiting card between them.

The focus of the great bath was a tank nearly 40 feet long and eight feet deep. A veranda surrounded the tank, and colonnades supported a roof sheltering small rooms for dignitaries to bathe in privacy.

Still solid after centuries of use and 4,000 years of neglect, the central tank still retains its even, sloping floor and both of the staircases bathers once used to descend into it from either end.

A slender-stemmed vessel of fired clay
—one of several that have turned up in
the excavations in the vicinity of
Moenjo-Daro's great bath—may have
been used to hold libations during
sacred rituals; vessels of similar design
crop up in Mesopotamian graves.

Triangular cakes of baked clay, thought
to have been used as scrubbers by
those who performed their ablutions in
the great bath, still retain their
abrasive surfaces. The top one was
etched with a crosshatch pattern,
before firing, for added roughness.

A Vault for Community Wealth

A symbol of Moenjo-Daro's wealth and dominance over the provinces around it, the granary stood like a fortress on the citadel. In the city's most prosperous days, around 2000 B.C., the granary had much the look of a modern bank—and perhaps a similar function. It may have been the official repository of wheat and barley raised on the neighboring plains and brought to town by farmers; the government would have used the grain to pay craftsmen and workers for their wares and services.

A drawing of the granary shows its loading dock, a 150-foot porch with a bay where carts could deposit produce. Grain was stored in the wooden superstructure, shown cut away in the right portion to reveal underfloor ducts that allowed air to circulate.

Discovered in a shambles of tumbled masonry, the granary's once-awesome walls now rise only a few feet above the ground.

A grain-storage jar is adorned with a leaf design typical of much Moenjo-Daro pottery. Jars were used for grain storage because they kept their perishable contents dry and, equally important, safe from various pests.

Bullock-drawn carts such as this one —actually a toy version in terra cotta —were used to haul grain jars; the wooden staves held the jars in place. Similarly constructed carts are still used for the same purpose in Pakistan.

A Design for Neatness

The grid pattern on which the city was laid out and the precision of the building methods attest to the order that characterizes Moenjo-Daro. But regular planning was only one aspect of a general passion for neatness, for the people insisted on cleanliness. Many private houses had interior wells and rooms for bathing, even though there was a splendid public bathing place at their disposal; and the sewer system, which was extensive and complex, was kept in good repair by municipal workers.

An excavator's map of a portion of the lower city discloses the planners' rational scheme: Moenjo-Daro's main artery, such as the avenue at right, ran north-south with narrow lanes off it.

Thirty feet wide and lined with ruined houses that once may have had shops in front, this avenue was the main thoroughfare through Moenjo-Daro's residential area, located below the citadel.

A household privy (below) and the chute outlets (bottom) that once conveyed bath water or rain runoff to municipal drainage conduits testify to the excellence of Moenjo-Daro's sanitation system.

The arched roof of what may have been an underground duct for fresh water stands exposed after excavation (below). Used water from houses drained into large sewer lines like the one at bottom.

A Home for Comfort

The upper-class residents of Moenjo-Daro enjoyed a good life. Large, well-built villas housed them in comfort and high style. A typical rich man's home, such as the one shown in an artist's reconstruction below, had lodgings for several servants, an interior courtyard, a fine downstairs guest room which offered privacy, a whole upper story for the family's bedrooms and, of course, a well that provided fresh water for an interior plumbing system.

A ground-level courtyard was the center of this two-story house; passageways off it led to a guest chamber (left), to quarters for servants (right) and to a well (bottom). A stairway gave access to family bedrooms upstairs.

Steps and stout brick walls, some of them five feet thick, are all that remain of what must once have been the grand house of a wealthy citizen or high state official.

A useful household item, this undecorated cup of fired clay was probably used for drinking water. Its disk-shaped, pierced handle suggests that its owner may have kept it hanging by a thong near his well for quick refreshment.

An ancient precursor of the modern baby bottle, this ceramic feeding cup is made with a wide mouth to be filled from the top and a long spout through which an infant could suck fluids; cups of similar design are still used by peasant mothers in Pakistan.

The Emergence of Man

This chart records the progression of life on earth from its first appearance in the warm waters of the new-formed planet through the evolution of man himself; it traces his physical, social, technological and intellectual development to the Christian era. To place these advances in commonly used chronological sequences, the column at the

Geology	Archeology	Billions of Years Ago	
Precambrian earliest era		**4.5**	Creation of the Earth
		4	Formation of the primordial sea
		3	First life, single-celled algae and bacteria, appears in water
		2	
		1	

Geology	Archeology	Millions of Years Ago	
			First oxygen-breathing animals appear
		800	
			Primitive organisms develop interdependent specialized cells
Paleozoic ancient life		**600**	Shell-bearing multicelled invertebrate animals appear
			Evolution of armored fish, first animals to possess backbones
		400	Small amphibians venture onto land
			Reptiles and insects arise
			Thecodont, ancestor of dinosaurs, arises
Mesozoic middle life		**200**	Age of dinosaurs begins
			Birds appear
			Mammals live in shadow of dinosaurs
			Age of dinosaurs ends
		80	
			Prosimians, earliest primates, develop in trees
Cenozoic recent life		**60**	
		40	Monkeys and apes evolve
		20	
		10	Ramapithecus, oldest known primate with apparently manlike traits, evolves in India and Africa
		8	
		6	Australopithecus, closest primate ancestor to man, appears in Africa
		4	

Geology	Archeology	Millions of Years Ago	
Lower Pleistocene oldest period of most recent epoch	**Lower Paleolithic** oldest period of Old Stone Age	**2**	Oldest known tool fashioned by man in Africa
			First true man, Homo erectus, emerges in East Indies and Africa
		1	Homo erectus populates temperate zones

Geology	Archeology	Thousands of Years Ago	
Middle Pleistocene middle period of most recent epoch		**800**	Man learns to control and use fire
		600	
			Large-scale, organized elephant hunts staged in Europe
		400	Man begins to make artificial shelters from branches
		200	
Upper Pleistocene latest period of most recent epoch	**Middle Paleolithic** middle period of Old Stone Age		Neanderthal man emerges in Europe
		80	
		60	Ritual burials in Europe and Near East suggest belief in afterlife
			Woolly mammoths hunted by Neanderthals in northern Europe
		40	Cave bear becomes focus of cult in Europe
	Upper Paleolithic latest period of Old Stone Age		Cro-Magnon man arises in Europe
			Asian hunters cross Bering Land Bridge to populate New World
			Oldest known written record, lunar notations on bone, made in Europe
			Man reaches Australia
			First artists decorate walls and ceilings of caves in France and Spain
		30	Figurines sculpted for nature worship
		20	Invention of needle makes sewing possible
			Bison hunting begins on Great Plains of North America
Holocene present epoch	**Mesolithic** Middle Stone Age	**10**	Bow and arrow invented in Europe
			Pottery first made in Japan

(vertical label along left of Upper Pleistocene/Paleolithic column: **Last Ice Age**)

▼ Four billion years ago ▼ Three billion years ago

▲ Origin of the Earth (4.5 billion)   ▲ First life (3.5 billion)

far left of each of the chart's four sections identifies the great geological eras into which the earth's history is divided by scientists, while the second column lists the archeological ages of human history. The key dates in the rise of life and of man's outstanding accomplishments appear in the third column (years and events mentioned in this volume of The Emergence of Man appear in bold type). The chart is not to scale; the reason is made clear by the bar below, which represents in linear scale the 4.5 billion years spanned by the chart—on the scaled bar, the portion relating to the total period of known human existence (far right) is too small to be distinguished.

Geology	Archeology	Years B.C.	
Holocene (cont.)	Neolithic New Stone Age	9000	
			Sheep domesticated in Near East
			Dog domesticated in North America
		8000	**Jericho, oldest known city, settled**
			Goat domesticated in Persia
			Man cultivates his first crops, wheat and barley, in Near East
		7000	Pattern of village life grows in Near East
			Catal Hüyük, in what is now Turkey, becomes largest Neolithic city
			Loom invented in Near East
			Cattle domesticated in Near East
		6000	Agriculture begins to replace hunting in Europe
	Copper Age		**Copper used in trade in Mediterranean area**
			Corn cultivated in Mexico
		4000	Sail-propelled boats used in Egypt
			Oldest known massive stone monument built in Brittany
			First city-states develop in Sumer
			Cylinder seals begin to be used as marks of identification in Near East
		3500	First potatoes grown in South America
			Wheel originates in Sumer
			Man begins to cultivate rice in Far East
			Silk moth domesticated in China
			Egyptian merchant trading ships start to ply the Mediterranean
			First writing, pictographic, composed in Near East
	Bronze Age	3000	Bronze first used to make tools in Near East
			City life spreads to Nile Valley
			Plow is developed in Near East
			Accurate calendar based on stellar observation devised in Egypt
			Pyramids built in Egypt
			Minoan navigators begin to venture into seas beyond the Mediterranean
		2600	**Variety of gods and heroes glorified in Gilgamesh and other epics in Near East**
		2500	**Cities rise in the Indus Valley**

Geology	Archeology	Years B.C.	
Holocene (cont.)	Bronze Age (cont.)	2400	Stonehenge, most famous of ancient stone monuments, begun in England
			Earliest written code of laws drawn up in Sumer
		2000	Chicken and elephant domesticated in Indus Valley
			Use of bronze spreads to Europe
			Eskimo culture begins in Bering Strait area
			Herdsmen of Central Asia learn to tame and ride horses
		1500	Invention of ocean-going outrigger canoes enables man to reach islands of South Pacific
			Ceremonial bronze sculptures created in China
			Imperial government, ruling distant provinces, established by Hittites
	Iron Age	1400	Iron in use in Near East
			First complete alphabet devised in script of the Ugarit people in Syria
			Hebrews introduce concept of monotheism
		1000	Reindeer domesticated in Eurasia
		900	Phoenicians develop modern alphabet
		800	Celtic culture begins to spread use of iron throughout Europe
			Nomads create a far-flung society based on the horse in Russian steppes
			First highway system built in Assyria
			Homer composes Iliad and Odyssey
		700	Rome founded
			Wheel barrow invented in China
		200	Epics about India's gods and heroes, the Mahabharata and Ramayana, written
			Water wheel invented in Near East
		0	Christian era begins

▼ Two billion years ago   ▼ One billion years ago

First oxygen-breathing animals (900 million) ▲   First animals to possess ▲ backbones (470 million)   First men (1.3 million) ▲

Credits

The sources for the illustrations in this book are shown below. Credits from left to right are separated by semicolons, from top to bottom by dashes.

Cover—Painting by Burt Silverman, background photograph by Emmett Bright, 8,9—Hilprecht Collection (Inez Bernhardt) Jena University. 12,13—Map by Rafael D. Palacios, color indication by George V. Kelvin. 16,17—Map by Rafael D. Palacios; Mrs. James Mellaart; Courtesy University Museum, University of Pennsylvania—Aldo Durazzi courtesy Archaeological Museum, Heraklion, Crete. 18—From *Palestine Exploration Quarterly,* January-June 1966, courtesy Diana Kirkbride—Mrs. James Mellaart. 21 through 27—Courtesy Clifford C. Lamberg-Karlovsky, Peabody Museum of Archaeology and Ethnology, Harvard University. 28—Jericho Excavation Fund. 30,31—Courtesy The New York Public Library, Spencer Collection. 33—Aerofilms Ltd.—Jericho Excavation Fund. 34—David Rubinger. 36 through 40—Jericho Excavation Fund. 42—Mrs. James Mellaart. 46,47—Mrs. James Mellaart. 48,49—From *Catal Huyuk* by James Mellaart; Copied from an original drawing by James Mellaart. 51—Copied from an original drawing by James Mellaart. 52—Ara Guler courtesy Ankara Archaeological Museum; Mrs. James Mellaart. 53—Mrs. James Mellaart; Ara Guler courtesy Ankara Archaeological Museum; Mrs. James Mellaart. 54—Mrs. James Mellaart. 56—Ara Guler courtesy Ankara Archaeological Museum. 57—Ara Guler courtesy Ankara Archaeological Museum, except right top and bottom, Mrs. James Mellaart. 58—Ara Guler courtesy Ankara Archaeological Museum. 61 through 67—Paintings by Michael A. Hampshire, photographs by Mrs. James Mellaart. 68—Jericho Excavation Fund. 70 through 73—Mrs. James Mellaart. 74,75—Alex Efty courtesy The Cyprus Museum, Nicosia. 76,77—Mrs. James Mellaart. 78—Jericho Excavation Fund—Mrs. James Mellaart. 81 through 87—Paintings by Jack Endewelt. 88—Lee Boltin courtesy University Museum, University of Pennsylvania. 90—Hirmer Fotoarchiv, Munich. 93—Courtesy of the Trustees of the British Museum, London. 95—From *Sumer* by André Parrot, University Museum, University of Pennsylvania (British Museum). 96—Aldo Durazzi courtesy National Museum, Damascus. 98—Courtesy University Museum, University of Pennsylvania. 100—Courtesy of the Trustees of the British Museum, London; Hirmer Fotoarchiv, Munich. 101—Hirmer Fotoarchiv, Munich; Archives Photographiques. 103—Courtesy of the Oriental Institute, University of Chicago. 107—Courtesy University Museum, University of Pennsylvania. 108,109—Hirmer Fotoarchiv, Munich; From *Ur* by Eva Strommenger, Hirmer Fotoarchiv, Munich. 111—Aldo Durazzi courtesy Aleppo Museum. 112—Dmitri Kessel courtesy Musée du Louvre, Paris. 113—Francis Bartlett Donation of 1912. Courtesy Museum of Fine Arts, Boston; Aldo Durazzi courtesy The Iraqi Museum, Baghdad. 114,115—Dmitri Kessel courtesy Musée du Louvre, Paris. 116,117—Aldo Durazzi courtesy The Iraqi Museum, Baghdad; Courtesy of the Trustees of the British Museum, London. 118—Hirmer Fotoarchiv, Munich. 119—Courtesy of the Trustees of the British Museum, London; Cliché Réunion des Musées Nationaux. 120—Courtesy of the Trustees of the British Museum, London. 121—Courtesy University Museum, University of Pennsylvania; Aldo Durazzi courtesy The Iraqi Museum, Baghdad. 122—George F. Dales courtesy University Museum, University of Pennsylvania. 125—Emmett Bright courtesy National Museum of Pakistan, Karachi, except bottom left, Aldo Durazzi courtesy The Iraqi Museum, Baghdad. 126—Larry Burrows, TIME-LIFE Picture Agency, © 1961 Time Incorporated courtesy National Museum of Pakistan, Karachi. 128—Emmett Bright courtesy National Museum of Pakistan, Karachi. 129—Emmett Bright courtesy National Museum of Pakistan, Karachi; Jehangir Gazdar courtesy National Museum, New Delhi. 131—Jehangir Gazdar courtesy National Museum, New Delhi. 132—Emmett Bright courtesy National Museum of Pakistan, Karachi. 133—Aldo Durazzi courtesy The Iraqi Museum, Baghdad. 134—Jehangir Gazdar courtesy National Museum, New Delhi. 136—Jehangir Gazdar courtesy National Museum, New Delhi, except bottom right, Emmett Bright courtesy National Museum of Pakistan, Karachi. 137—Jehangir Gazdar courtesy National Museum, New Delhi—Emmett Bright courtesy Archaeological Museum, Moenjo-Daro. 139—Larry Burrows, TIME-LIFE Picture Agency, © 1961 Time Incorporated courtesy National Museum of Pakistan, Karachi. 141—Courtesy Clifford C. Lamberg-Karlovsky, Peabody Museum of Archaeology and Ethnology, Harvard University. 142,143—Larry Burrows, TIME-LIFE Picture Agency, © 1961 Time Incorporated courtesy National Museum, New Delhi. 145—George F. Dales courtesy University Museum, University of Pennsylvania. 146,147—Drawing by Martin Weaver, from *Civilizations of the Indus Valley and Beyond* by Sir Mortimer Wheeler; Larry Burrows, TIME-LIFE Picture Agency, © 1961 Time Incorporated courtesy Department of Archaeology and Museums, Government of Pakistan; Larry Burrows, TIME-LIFE Picture Agency, © 1961 Time Incorporated courtesy National Museum of Pakistan, Karachi; Jehangir Gazdar courtesy National Museum, New Delhi. 148,149—Drawing by Martin Weaver, from *Civilizations of the Indus Valley and Beyond* by Sir Mortimer Wheeler; Larry Burrows, TIME-LIFE Picture Agency, © 1961 Time Incorporated courtesy Department of Archaeology and Museums, Government of Pakistan; Jehangir Gazdar courtesy National Museum, New Delhi—Emmett Bright courtesy Archaeological Museum, Moenjo-Daro. 150,151—From *Further Excavations at Moenjo-Daro* by E.J.H. MacKay, copyright The Archaeological Survey of India; Larry Burrows, TIME-LIFE Picture Agency, © 1961 Time Incorporated courtesy Department of Archaeology and Museums, Government of Pakistan except far top right, Roloff Beny courtesy Department of Archaeology and Museums, Government of Pakistan. 152,153—Drawing by Peter Pratt, from *Civilizations of the Indus Valley and Beyond* by Sir Mortimer Wheeler; Roloff Beny courtesy Department of Archaeology and Museums, Government of Pakistan; Larry Burrows, TIME-LIFE Picture Agency, © 1961 Time Incorporated courtesy National Museum of Pakistan, Karachi.

Acknowledgments

For the help given in the preparation of this book, the editors are indebted to Afral Ahmed, Curator, Archeological Museum, Moenjo-Daro; John Alexander, Senior Lecturer in Archeology, University of London; J. Lawrence Angel, Curator, Physical Anthropology, Smithsonian Institution; Robert D. Biggs, Professor of Assyriology, Oriental Institute, University of Chicago; Raffaele Biscione, Marcello Piperno, Maurizio Tosi (Scientific Director, Italian Archeological Mission to Iran), Giuseppe Tucci (President), Italian Institute of the Middle and Far East, Rome; Piero Cassoli, Director, Italian Institute of Human Paleontology, Rome; George F. Dales Jr., Professor of South Asian and Near Eastern Archeology, University of California, Berkeley; Department of Western Asiatic Antiquities, British Museum, London; Caroline Dosker, Assistant Registrar, Robert H. Dyson Jr., Professor of Anthropology and Curator, Near Eastern Section, Maude de Schauensee, Research Associate, Near Eastern Section, University Museum, and Ake W. Sjoberg, Curator of the Tablet Collection and Professor of Assyriology, University of Pennsylvania; Richard S. Ellis, Associate Professor of Near Eastern Archeology, Yale University; S. P. Gupta, Keeper, National Museum, and Dhanpai Rai, Technical Assistant, National Museum, New Delhi; Hans Peter Helbaek, Museum Conservator, National Museum, Copenhagen; Dame Kathleen M. Kenyon, Jericho Excavation Fund; Louise Mackie, Acting Chief Curator, Textile Museum, Washington, D.C.; Frederick R. Matson, Research Professor of

Archeology, Pennsylvania State University; James Mellaart, Lecturer in Anatolian Archeology, and David Oates, Professor of Western Asiatic Archeology, Institute of Archaeology, London; Gerhard Rudolf Meyer, Director General, Berlin State Museums, Berlin; A. S. Naqui, Director General of Antiquities, Karachi; Kyriacos Nicolaou, Curator, Nicosia Archeological Museum, Cyprus; Robert L. Raikes, Raikes and Partners, Rome; Fawzi Rashid, Director, Iraq Museum, Baghdad; Niaz Rasool, Director, National Museum of Pakistan, Karachi; Colin Renfrew, Professor of Archeology, University of Southampton, England; David Rubinger, Jerusalem, Israel; Issa Salman, Director General of Antiquities, Baghdad; Shawqi Shaath, Director, Archeological Museum, Aleppo, Syria; Françoise Talon, Researcher, Department of Oriental Antiquities, Louvre, Paris; Suleyman Tawfig, Director General of Antiquities, Damascus, Syria; Ian A. Todd, Assistant Professor of Archeology, Brandeis University; Maurits N. van Loon, Professor of Archeology and Pre-history of Western Asia, Institute of Pre- and Proto-history, University of Amsterdam; Sir Mortimer Wheeler, Professor of Ancient History, British Academy, London; Bachir Zouhdi, Curator, Archeological Museum, Aleppo.

Bibliography

Urban Evolution and Excavations

Braidwood, Robert J. and Gordon R. Willey, eds., *Courses Toward Urban Life.* Aldine Publishing Co., 1962.

Edwards, I.E.S., C. J. Gadd and N.G.L. Hammond, eds., *The Cambridge Ancient History,* Vol. 1, Part 1 & 2. Cambridge University Press, 1971.

Jacobs, Jane, *The Economy of Cities.* Random House, 1969.

Lamberg-Karlovsky, C. C., ed., *Old World Archaeology: Foundations of Civilization.* W. H. Freeman and Co., 1972.

Mallowan, M.E.L., *Early Mesopotamia and Iran.* McGraw-Hill Book Co., 1965.

Mellaart, James, *Earliest Civilizations of the Near East.* McGraw-Hill, 1965.

Shapiro, Harry L., ed., *Man, Culture and Society.* Oxford University Press, 1971.

Ucko, Peter J., Ruth Tringham and G. W. Dimbleby, *Man, Settlement and Urbanism.* Duckworth, 1972.

Jericho

Kenyon, Kathleen M., *Archaeology in the Holy Land.* Praeger, 1970.

Digging up Jericho. Ernest Benn Limited, 1957.

Catal Hüyük

Mellaart, James A., *Catal Hüyük: A Neolithic Town in Anatolia.* McGraw-Hill Book Co., 1967.

Pearson, Kenneth and Patricia Connor, *The Dorak Affair.* Atheneum, 1968.

Domestic Arts

Albright, W. F., *The Archaeology of Palestine.* Pelican, 1960.

Kenyon, Kathleen M., *Royal Cities of the Old Testament.* Schocken Books, 1971.

Matson, Frederick R., ed., *Ceramics and Man.* Aldine, 1965.

Sangar, N. K., *Prehistoric Art in Europe.* Penguin Books, 1968.

Weir, Shelagh, *Spinning and Weaving in Palestine.* The British Museum, 1970.

Sumer

Adams, Robert McC., *The Evolution of Urban Society.* Aldine-Atherton, 1966.

Bottéro, Jean, Elena Cassin and Jean Vercoutter, eds., *The Near East: The Early Civilizations.* Delacorte Press, 1967.

Ehrich, Robert W., ed., *Chronologies in Old World Archaeology.* The University of Chicago Press, 1965.

Frankfort, Henri, *The Art and Architecture of the Ancient Orient.* Penguin Books, 1963.

Frankfort, H. and H. A., John A. Wilson, Thorkild Jacobsen, William A. Irwin, *The Intellectual Adventure of Ancient Man.* The University of Chicago Press, 1967.

Jacobsen, Thorkild, *Toward the Image of Tammuz and Other Essays on Mesopotamian History and Culture,* ed. by William L. Moran. Harvard University Press, 1970.

Jones, Tom, ed., *The Sumerian Problem.* John Wiley and Sons, Inc., 1969.

Kramer, Samuel Noah, *History Begins at Sumer.* Doubleday and Co., Inc., 1959.

Sumerian Mythology. Harper and Row, 1961.

The Sumerians. The University of Chicago Press, 1963.

Lloyd, Seton, *The Art of the Ancient Near East.* Frederick A. Praeger, 1961.

Oppenheim, A. Leo, *Ancient Mesopotamia.* The University of Chicago Press, 1964.

Parrot, André, *Sumer: The Dawn of Art.* Golden Press, 1961.

Pritchard, James B., *The Ancient Near East in Pictures Relating to the Old Testament.* Princeton University Press, 1954.

Pritchard, James B., ed., *Ancient Near Eastern Texts Relating to the Old Testament.* Princeton University Press, 1950.

Roux, Georges, *Ancient Iraq.* Penguin Books, 1964.

Saggs, H.W.F., *The Greatness that was Babylon.* Praeger, 1969.

Singer, Charles, E. J. Holmyard and A. R. Hall, eds., *A History of Technology,* Vol. I. Oxford University Press, 1967.

Indus Civilization

Fairservis, Walter A., Jr., *The Roots of Ancient India.* Macmillan, 1971.

Mackay, E.J.H., *Further Excavations at Mohenjo-Daro.* Government of India Press, 1938.

Piggott, Stuart, *The Dawn of Civilization.* Thames and Hudson, 1961.

Wheeler, Sir Mortimer, *Civilizations of the Indus Valley and Beyond.* Thames and Hudson, 1966.

The Indus Civilization. Cambridge University Press, 1968.

Index